Surprised by God

Other outstanding books by Stan Gaede:

Life in the Slow Lane: The Benefits of Not Getting What you Want When You Want It

For All Who Have Been Forsaken

Belonging: Our Need for Community in Church and Family

Where Gods May Dwell: Understanding the Human Condition

Surprised by God

Big Lessons from the Little Things in Life

STAN GAEDE

ZondervanPublishingHouse
Grand Rapids, Michigan

A Division of HarperCollinsPublishers

Surprised by God
Copyright © 1993 by S. D. Gaede

Requests for information should be addressed to
Zondervan Publishing House
Grand Rapids, Michigan 49530

Library of Congress Cataloging-in-Publication Data

Gaede, S. D.
   Surprised by God : big lessons from the little things in life / Stan Gaede.
     p. cm.
   ISBN 0-310-58671-2 (pbk.)
   1. Spiritual life—Christianity. 2. Gaede, S. D. I. Title.
  BV4501.2.G275   1993
  248.4—dc20   92-2461
                                            CIP

Edited by Bob Hudson
Cover design and illustration by David Marty

Printed in the United States of America

93 94 95 96 97 98 / DH / 10 9 8 7 6 5 4 3 2 1

To Nathaniel with love,
who, like his grandfather
is tall

CONTENTS

INTRODUCTION

My life has been a series of surprises. They have often been the source of embarrassment to me, if not total humiliation. At other times they have been the basis of gratitude and rejoicing. But always they have been the occasion for God to break into my world—busting up my plans and expectations—to teach me what it means to be one of his children. The lessons have not been easy. And I'm a slow learner. But they involve some of the most significant and difficult issues faced by Christians today. Ultimately, it was because of their importance that I decided to commit them to paper.

Those who have read my previous book *Life in the Slow Lane* are already familiar with the way God works in my life. For first-time readers, all you need to know is that I'm a Boomer who grew up on a farm in California, met my wife, Judy, while attending a small Christian college in Santa Barbara during the sixties, after which we both went to graduate school—first in Southern California and then back east—and finally, settled in New England where I assumed the life of a college professor. Along the way, God blessed us with three children—Heather, Nathaniel, and Kirsten—and we've been paying the price ever since. Though neither book is intended to be exactly chronological, *Slow Lane* focused on our earlier years in California while *Surprised by God* begins with our departure for graduate school back east.

If this is your first encounter with my writing, don't worry. *Surprised by God* can be read independently—that's because my story is not really the point of this book, God is. And while I am undeniably this book's subject, I am not its object.

If you have already mastered the arts of

INTRODUCTION

knowing the Lord's will for your life
knowing what you need and who you are in God's eyes
knowing how to live, what to believe, and how to love
knowing the point of church or the meaning of success

then you probably have no reason to continue reading. But if my questions are yours, and my ignorance reflects your own, then perhaps my stories are your stories as well. And together, in these pages, we can be *Surprised by God*.

CHAPTER 1
DISCOVERING THE LORD'S WILL

THE LORD'S WILL

In June of 1971, Judy and I graduated from what I will call "Blah University." She received her California teaching certificate, and I received a master of arts degree in sociology. With four degrees and eleven years of higher education between us—not to mention mounting debts and mounting anxiety—one would have thought we were ready to begin contributing to society.

But contributions are not easy to make, especially if you are finicky about where to make them. The problem, you should know, was not Judy's. Her practicum in graduate school had conclusively shown that she and kindergartners were made for each other. Indeed, before she had even finished college, she was offered a plum position in one of the finest schools in the area. Judy, in other words, was ready to contribute.

I was another matter. I had decided to focus on a subfield within sociology for which a master's degree was little more than a pat on the back. It gave one a nice feeling but not much else. I discovered, moreover, that I enjoyed my subject. The deeper I went, the more interesting the questions became. And the more apparent it was that I would need a Ph.D. For intellectual as well as practical reasons, I knew I had to continue my parasitic career as a student.

The question was, where? For Judy, this was not an earthshaking problem. She was willing to go wherever the Lord led us, which, translated, meant that she was willing to set her career aspirations aside temporarily for the sake of mine.

I felt guilty about that, not just because it didn't seem quite fair, but also because the Lord had opened up a graduate school possibility back east, an opening that coincided remarkably well with my own hopes and dreams. To assuage my guilt, therefore, I came up with a plan. Not just any plan, but a Grand Plan. I would go to Preppie University back east where, in the span of about three years, I would secure the Ph.D. During that time, Judy would support us by locating a job as a kindergarten teacher somewhere near the university. After grad school we would take a year off, travel to Europe, roam wherever our little hearts desired, make a baby in a chalet somewhere in the Alps, and return home to begin our family as well as our careers.

Unfortunately, we made the baby in a sleazy motel room in San Jose instead. In the middle of suburbia. Just three months before we were supposed to take off for Preppie University. And three entire years before we were planning to take off for Europe. Now, San Jose is a nice town. Many people know the way there and not a few of them have taken advantage of that knowledge. But it is not the Alps. And a motel room is not a chalet. And these suburbs were definitely not in Europe. And life is not fair.

How did it happen? Well, that's another story. For now, all you need to know is that we enjoyed making this baby, despite the environment. You should also know that we had no intention of making a baby at the time. I don't know about other couples, but there seem to be two recurring themes in our baby-making experiences. One, we are never thinking about making babies when we actually make them. And two, we are always more than a little surprised by their arrival as a result.

That was especially the case with our first. For not only did this pregnancy throw our trip to Europe out the window, it also threw my entire future into question. The plan, remember, was to have Judy support us while I went to graduate school. The question now became, how could I afford to attend a fabulously

CHAPTER 1

expensive university for three years and survive with a family at the same time? Was further education even possible? Was it the right thing to do? Could it be that the Lord was trying to tell me something about my own aspirations? Could it be that I was heading down the wrong path altogether?

I didn't think so, but I had little evidence to the contrary. Or more accurately, the evidence could be interpreted in a variety of ways. On the one hand, I had done well in graduate school and enjoyed my subject. So a career as a scholar seemed an appropriate choice. On the other hand, there was no reason to go back east to achieve that objective. I had been accepted by a fine university in Southern California. Why not stay home, close to family and friends and known employment possibilities, to help us through the baby-having years? Why leave those you need when you know you're going to be needy?

Then again, the program at Preppie University was ideally suited to my needs. Graduate programs move in certain directions, and graduate students either move with the program or they are in danger of not moving at all. I knew that going to Preppie U would take me along one path and staying in Southern California would shove me in another. And the direction of Preppie U seemed much better suited to my interests and abilities. Still, did I know enough about either school to make that judgment? Did I know enough about myself? Wasn't it possible that I could go in either direction and be happy? Was it really so crucial to go back east?

And what about Judy—who honestly said, "Do whatever you think is best," and meant it—what about her? What would be best for my wife? She was a Southern Californian, after all, from her sunny disposition to her perpetually tanned toes. She had worked at Disneyland, for Pete's sake! Would she be happy back east? Was it fair to take her away from family, friends, and freeways, especially when she was about to give birth to our first child? I was no therapist, but it didn't take too much psychological insight to know that removing a pregnant woman from her support network six months before delivery wasn't the most

14

generous thing in the world to do. Was it fair to put my career ambitions ahead of her emotional needs?

The answer, obviously, was no. And yet, I knew she genuinely wanted me to make the decision that was best for my career. Judy was not difficult to read. If there had been any doubt in her mind, I would have known it. There was a sense in which it would have been disingenuous—even paternalistic—for me to make a decision for her sake when she was asking me to make it for mine. Didn't I honor her most by doing what she asked? And wasn't she honestly asking me to make the decision based on my own interests?

To such questions, there seemed no end. And no definitive answer. In every alternative, there was merit as well as guilt. And in every option, there was joy as well as pain.

In such circumstances, one is left to ponder the Lord's will. Especially if one is evangelical. "What do you want me to do, Lord?" is a question I must have asked at least a thousand times. And that question led to other, more perplexing questions

"You were the one who opened up the possibility of going to Preppie University, Lord. You know I couldn't have gotten in without a miracle on your part. Does that mean we should move back east?

"But you are also the author of Creation, not merely the admissions director of graduate schools. You are the one who gave us this little baby. And you gave it to us now. Why did you do that, Lord? Are you trying to tell me something? Is this an indication that I'm moving in the wrong direction? Should I continue in grad school in Southern California? Should I even pursue further education? Or would it be wise just to find the best job I can and begin supporting my family for a change?"

The questions were interminable. But even more perplexing was the fact that always—always, always—there were no clear-cut answers. The minute I thought I had a solution, some event or

CHAPTER 1

person would come along to render my judgment useless. Or silly. Or just plain wrong.

One evening Judy and I were driving across town to spend the evening with friends. I had pretty much decided that in spite of the hurdles that lay in our path, we should continue with our plans to move back east. All the arrangements had been made. Judy seemed eager to make the move. I had also made some feeble attempts to land a job at one of the local junior colleges in Southern California, and—to my delight—none of them were the least bit interested. And the more I looked into the graduate program at the local university, the more convinced I became that it was not well suited to my needs.

"Judy," I said as we whizzed along the freeway, "I think we should stick with our original idea and move back east. I was talking with Joe Shmoe—"

"Stan . . ." Judy tried to intervene.

"You know Joe, don't you?" I continued unabated. "He was at Blah the first year we were there? Anyway, he's in the doctoral program at Laid Back University now, and he says that their real strengths are in criminology and gerontology. Not social theory. It just—"

"Uh, Stan . . ."

"—well, it just doesn't seem wise to pursue studies there if they don't really excel in my areas of interest. I mean, I'm not planning a career as a criminal, after all, and I don't see myself being an advisor to the FBI on justice matters. Gerontology doesn't really interest me either. I mean—"

"Stan, I think . . ."

"—I mean, I like old people and all of that. But studying them? I don't think so. The elderly are to be revered and respected and enjoyed—and you know I do all of that—but I don't want to spend my life focusing on just one population. I mean—"

"Stan! Would you shut up and pull over? I think I'm going to be sick!"

As we careened to the side of the freeway, Judy was already

16

opening the car door. The wind was blowing briskly that evening, so as the door swung out, the breeze swung in, along with all the sights, sounds, and smells of sickness.

It was a mess, to say the least. But it was nothing compared to the mess I felt inside. For here was my wife, enduring the first few months of pregnancy, spilling her guts on the side of the road as a result, and what was I doing? Thinking about my career, that's what. Making my plans, based on my interests, and assuming therefore that it must be the Lord's will.

What a jerk I am! I thought to myself, as I rubbed Judy's back with one hand and cleaned up the car with the other. *What a self-centered jerk! This woman, not my career, is my first responsibility. How can I think of taking her away at a time like this? So what if the local university's program isn't perfect. I'll adapt. The Lord has given me a wife and family. And the Lord obviously wants me to put their needs before my own. We can't leave home now.*

"JUDY," I screamed as we moved back onto the freeway, both of us with our heads sticking out the window, desperately trying to retrieve as much fresh air as possible, "I THINK WE SHOULD JUST STAY HERE. . . ."

A truck whizzed by, nearly decapitating me. I thought about pulling my head back in the car. All things considered, however, decapitation seemed worth the risk.

". . . THIS IS NO TIME TO LEAVE OUR FAMILIES," I continued to yell. "YOU'LL WANT YOUR MOM AND DAD AROUND WHEN THE BABY COMES."

A fellow in a Rabbit convertible pulled up beside me and pinned me with his eyes, incredulity written all over his face. I realized that I looked pretty stupid, yelling like this with my head out the window. But again, I didn't really see any alternative. I continued my discussion.

"I JUST CAN'T BELIEVE THE LORD WANTS US TO MOVE 2,500 MILES FROM HOME AT A TIME LIKE THIS. I THINK WE SHOULD STAY!"

I began to feel sick. Judy must have sensed my despair because she grabbed my free hand and held it tightly while she pulled her head back in the car and reclined comfortably in the seat. The color had returned to her face, and it was hard to imagine that just ten minutes earlier she had been one of the wretched of the earth. She looked beautiful.

"As I recall, Stan," she said softly, "just a few minutes ago—when I was trying to get you to pull the car over to the side of the road—you said that the Lord wanted us to move back east. Now you say he doesn't. What made the Lord change his mind so quickly do you suppose?"

The words could have been mean spirited, but they weren't. She said it with a smile and a gentle tone. She was doing nothing more than reminding me that I was altering my opinion—and blaming the Lord for my own double-mindedness.

"Don't make a decision right now," she continued. "Let's see our friends this evening and try to have a good time. You see if you can forget about this decision. I'll try to forget about being sick. And maybe we'll both have clearer heads in the morning."

It was good advice. And as I gave Judy's hand a squeeze, I began to relax for the first time in weeks. But even as I relaxed, I realized that Judy's query had raised an even more perplexing question than the one concerning our future destination.

What is the Lord's will, anyway? And how are we ever to find it?

THE LORD'S WILL NOT

I was still asking that question as we headed into Fort Smith, Arkansas, just two days after leaving California for the East. We had not so much made a decision to go to Preppie University as we had *not* made a decision *not* to go. Inertia, not reason, had become the primary mover. And as we crossed the state line into Arkansas a little before midnight—with our U-Haul truck, our cat, and our VW van trailing along behind—I was not convinced we had made the right choice.

It was August for one thing. And from Needles to Oklahoma City we had encountered nothing but heat. The sun was only one of many disappointments, however. Our truck, which looked brand new and held a good deal of furniture, was getting about two miles per gallon and drove like . . . well, like a truck. I don't know why that should have been a surprise. I had driven trucks all my life on my dad's farm. But for some reason, I had assumed that the U-Haul people had figured out a way to take the truckiness out of trucks. They hadn't. And it was a major effort just to herd the thing down the freeway without running over motorcycles, hitchhikers, or whatever else came within fifty yards of our vehicle. Of course, it goes without saying that the truck lacked air-conditioning.

Our cat was not pleased with the truck either. Talcott began the ride on Judy's lap, assuming the truck was something like our

CHAPTER 1

VW van. The minute I turned over the engine, however, his ears reached for the sky, and his whole body began to stiffen. A mile down the road, he started pacing across our laps. By the time we hit twelfth gear, Talcott was under the seat, coiled in a prenatal position and howling like a dog. We finally had to stop the truck and throw him in the van, even though we knew he would probably fillet our down pillows and hold us accountable for the rest of our lives. But I just couldn't take the heat, the truck, and a howling cat at the same time.

As we crossed into Fort Smith, then, we were pretty tired. Trying to save money, we had only made one prolonged stop the entire trip, that being an eight-hour sleep-over in Albuquerque. As my eyelids increased in poundage, saving money seemed like a progressively unimportant aspiration. The truck, now moving on its own, made a beeline for the next exit, and we soon found ourselves heading down a two-lane country road, straight for the bright lights of Fort Smith, straight for the most comfortable motel in town.

Not long before we crossed the city limits, though, I began to notice something peculiar in my rearview mirror. It was a vehicle, not unlike any other, but strange in one respect: It maintained a discreet distance between itself and our truck. That was unusual for a number of reasons. First, people don't like to follow trucks. They either speed around them, or if that's not possible, they fall back and let the truck move on ahead. This fellow didn't do either of those two things, and that was the second strange thing. He just sat there, about twenty-five yards behind my truck and maintained his position perfectly. I mean perfectly. And that's a hard thing to do even in the best of circumstances. But this was not the best of circumstances; this was a country road in Arkansas!

This continued for a couple of miles, and not being a particularly patient man on the highway anyway, I began to get annoyed. *What in the world is wrong with him?* I thought. I was too tired to come up with an answer, so I decided to just get rid of the problem. Slowly, I began taking my foot off the accelerator, letting my speed fall back to 50. Then 45. Now 40. And eventually down to 35 miles per hour. Follower didn't miss a beat, maintaining his distance with just as much precision as before. I hit the gas, bringing my speed up to nearly 70, but Follower remained undeterred, keeping his place a safe twenty-five yards behind.

"What the honk is he doing?" I now blurted out to my sleepy wife. She paid no attention, assuming I was just in another one of my combat moods on the highway.

I quickly had my answer, however. When we finally penetrated the city limits, the street lights brought Follower into clear relief. As I peered into my rearview mirror, Follower first took the shape of a car. Then a blue car. Then a blue car with a light on its roof. And finally a blue car with three sets of lights on its roof, a large hatted man at the wheel, a shotgun on its dashboard, and probably a bazooka and fifteen hand grenades on the front seat. It was, in other words, a Fort Smith policeman.

"Honey, . . . we've got trouble," I said in greatly hushed tones, even though I wasn't sure why.

"I know, Stan, I'm sleepy too. Just take the first motel that comes along."

"I'm not tired anymore, Judy. We've got a policeman following us, and he's been tailing me for at least five miles. I don't know what the problem is, but he's definitely not friendly."

"There's a motel, Stan," Judy said as she snapped to attention. "Let's pull in there."

I obeyed, even though the place looked like a cross between a stable and a house of ill repute. As I popped out of the truck and walked to the office, I passed a No Vacancy sign but found that hard to believe. How could a place like this be full? I asked.

But the man inside confirmed the sign. "Sorry, Son, we're full up tonight," he bellowed. "Big convention in town." Again, I found that hard to believe. What kind of convention would use a place like this? I wondered, as I made my way back to the truck. Pool Players of America? People for a Better Bowling Alley? My tiredness was starting to show. As well as my middle-class ethnocentrism.

"No luck," I said to Judy as I jumped back into the truck. "We'll have to find something a little pricier, I'm afraid."

As we headed back onto the road, I took a quick peek in my rearview mirror, knowing that we had ditched the policeman, but checking just to make sure. I was relieved to find that the spot twenty-five yards to our rear was now vacant. Only one car was behind us, and he was directly on our tail, no doubt anxious to get around us.

I pulled far to the right so he could pass us easily. Nothing happened. I thought it might help if I slowed down a bit, but that didn't have any effect either. I reached out the window and adjusted my mirror so that I could get a better look at the car.

"Judy," I said in a controlled scream, "Blue Bayou is still on our tail!"

Judy kept her mouth shut, trying to be a calming influence and at the same time find another motel sign. "We haven't done anything wrong, Stan. I don't think you ought to worry about it."

"Don't worry?" I blurted out. "Don't worry? My dear wife, it's past midnight. We're in Arkansas. We've got California license plates. We're pulling a VW van—affectionately known as a 'Hippie Wagon' in these parts. We've probably got sociologist written all over our faces. And Shotgun Sally is on our tail. And you say, 'Don't worry!' What is that supposed to mean, anyway? This is no time for faith. This is a time for fear. Let's face it, we're in trouble!"

As usual during such outbursts, Judy paid no attention, knowing that it would soon pass and knowing that my mouth had once again far outpaced my brain. "There's a Holiday Inn, Stan," she finally said. "Over there. Just around the corner."

Praise the Lord, I thought. Middle-class America! Regular people. Regular rooms. And regular prices (you can't have everything). The important thing is that we were finally on home turf. In a world we understood. In a world that was safe.

THE LORD'S WILL NOT

The sense of security did not last long, however. For again we were confronted by a No Vacancy sign and a man who said, "Sorry, Son. We're full up." At least it was nice to know that I had so many fathers in Arkansas.

"Are you sure you don't have anything at all?" I asked pleadingly. "We're very tired, and we've just got to find a place to stay."

"I'm sorry, young man. The Combined Society of Bowlers and Billiard Players has taken everything in town. We just don't have a thing."

I must have looked crestfallen because the man quickly followed up his assertion with a qualification. "Unless . . . unless your name is Rothen. I have a room reserved for a couple named Rothen, and they haven't shown up yet. You wouldn't happen to be them, would you?" he asked with a funny sort of smile.

"I'm afraid not," I moaned, as I started for the door.

"Are you sure you're not the Rothens?" he asked more firmly, his voice following me as I continued down the hall. "If you are, I can give you a room. No questions asked."

I started to yell out an incredulous *no* when I finally realized what he was doing. He had a room that the Rothens had reserved for the night. But it was almost one in the morning, and chances were great that the Rothens weren't going to use the room. He couldn't give the room to me since, if they showed up, he'd be in trouble. But if I said I was Mr. Rothen, he was in the clear, regardless of what happened.

It was a nice gesture, and I could see by his smile that he was hoping I would go along with it. And once I realized what he was saying, there wasn't anything in the world that I wanted more to do than say yes. I was tired. My nerves were shot. The world outside was a foreign land to me, full of dangers and evils that I could only imagine. And here, in this Holiday Inn, there was peace and comfort and rest. With every bone in my body, every fiber in my being, I wanted to say, "Yes, indeed. I am Mr. Rothen."

But there was another voice in my being, with another

answer, imprinted long ago—by a parent and then a Sunday school teacher and then by my own eyes in the quiet of my room. "Do not be deceitful" were the clear words of this voice. And their message was not at all ambiguous, nor their implications difficult to figure out.

"Uh . . . thanks. Thanks very much," I said in the kindest tone I could muster. "But I can't do that. I'm not Mr. Rothen . . . though I certainly wish I were. I'll see what we can find down the road."

"You won't find anything," the man responded quickly. "It's a weekend night with a convention in town. I doubt there's any vacancy within a twenty-mile radius of Fort Smith. I've got a room, Mr. Rothen. If you'll just sign here, it's yours."

So easy, I thought to myself. This would be so easy. And maybe even right as well. After all, it's dangerous to drive while you're tired. I've got a pregnant wife and an innocent cat to think about. Is it right to put them at risk on the road? Isn't a little lie here really the lesser of two evils? Wouldn't the Lord understand?

"Get thee behind me Satan," I mumbled as I walked toward the door, my mind still buzzing with possibilities.

"What's that?" the man asked, confused.

"Oh, nothing," I said with raised voice. "I was talking to someone else. Thanks for your help."

As I walked back to the truck, I felt angry, confused, and helpless, all at the same time. The one thing I should have felt—victorious—was nowhere in sight. Indeed, in my fear, I felt more like a loser. It seemed to me that circumstances and my God were letting me down. I was becoming discouraged. And more than a little worried.

"No luck, Hon. They're full as well. We're just going to have to keep looking," I said as I climbed back into the truck. The words totally contradicted my mood, however, as I doubted we would find anything. But I didn't know what else to say. Or do.

As I swung the truck back onto the road, I once more looked into my rearview mirror, again to be confronted by Blue Bayou.

Terror mixed with anger now and produced a strange concoction of incredulity.

"What is it with this guy anyway?" I finally burst out at my steering wheel. "Doesn't he have anything else to do, for heaven's sake? Are they so hard up for crime around here that they have to harass people with out-of-state license plates who are just trying to find a place to sleep? Maybe the guy's too fat to get out of his car, so he justifies his salary by following foreigners around, chewing tobacco, and saying intelligent things like 'good buddy' on his car radio! The guy's probably a total—"

My tirade was cut short by the appearance of a red light in my rearview mirror. I looked down at my speedometer and noticed that I was going nearly 40 in a 25 mile-an-hour zone.

"—the guy's probably a six-foot-four linebacker who's going to rip my arms out of their sockets and put me away for the rest of my life!"

What a stupid thing to do, I thought, as I watched the door of the police cruiser swing open, followed immediately by the largest German shepherd I have ever seen in my life. *Oh, great. I'm going to be mauled to pieces as well. That will be a fitting conclusion to the evening!* I slumped down in my seat, expecting the worst.

When The Worst finally climbed out of his car, he was about five-foot-nine, with wire-rimmed glasses, no more than 150 pounds on his frame and no less than fifty years to his age. He looked more like one of my professors than a police officer. I couldn't do anything but stare.

"Good evening, Son," he said politely. "May I have a look at your license please?"

This time I was more than pleased to be his offspring. "Yes, sir, Dad. I mean, sir. I mean . . . it's right here, sir. Just a minute, sir. Here you are, sir. Thank you, sir. Anything else . . ."

"Are you having difficulty finding a room for the night?" he broke in. "I understand rooms are pretty hard to come by in Fort Smith tonight. You might want to head down the road a bit and try a motel right off the freeway. They're less likely to be full on the weekend. Also, just two miles beyond the Fort Smith exit there's a very nice rest stop. You could park there and sleep in your van. It's well lit and pretty safe. I don't think anyone would give you any trouble there."

He stopped talking and looked intently at my license. Finally, he handed it back. "Anyway, I just wanted you to know—before you got back on the freeway—that the brake lights on your truck aren't working. I noticed it when you got off the freeway so I decided to follow you for a while, just to make sure no one bashed into you from behind. But I think you ought to have that taken care of as soon as possible, especially since you seem to vary your speed a great deal. It's just not safe. Have a good trip." And off he went, his German shepherd happily wagging his tail behind him.

When we arrived at the rest stop, I was still thanking the Lord for his mercy and apologizing for my attitude about Arkansas.

"You know, Judy, this is really a very beautiful part of the country, isn't it? The people are friendly and incredibly helpful. And just look at this rest stop. Heavens, it's a regular park, with miles of freshly mowed grass, a clean bathroom, and pine trees everywhere you look. In California, they'd declare this a state preserve and charge you fifty dollars just to look around. I think Arkansas is a grand place!"

I was still carrying on about the wonders of the South as we made our way back to the van, spread our sleeping bags out, and laid down for a few hours of rest. As I snuggled my way into a cozy position, I was so enthralled by our change of fortune that I couldn't even take the smile off my face. *Life really is wonderful,* I thought. *I mean, here we are, sleeping in the beautiful out of doors, and it isn't costing us a cent. This is the best of both worlds!*

My smile started to dissipate, however, as drops of water began to appear on my brow. No, it wasn't rain. It was sweat. Traveling along at 60 mph, I hadn't noticed the humidity. Or the fact that the air was almost perfectly still. Lying down in our van, it suddenly became evident that the night was warm, the air was thick, and breezes were nonexistent.

"Hum . . . this isn't so good, is it, Hon?" I got no response. Judy was already asleep. *Well,* I thought to myself, *maybe I can just tough it out.* But as I lay there, the beads of perspiration became more pronounced and a tinge of claustrophobia descended down my spine. I knew I was doomed.

In a desperate search for relief, I jumped out of the van, threw my sleeping bag on the grass, and collapsed vulnerably to the ground. Shuffling around to find a comfortable spot, I was only faintly aware of a rustling noise somewhere over my head. As the sound grow louder, I started to take heart. *'Tis the gentle stirring of a summer breeze,* thought I, and I eagerly awaited the first wafts of wind to collide gloriously with my perspiring body. *This will be a relief!*

Unfortunately, it wasn't a Southern breeze but a Southern mosquito that descended from the heavens. And it was accompanied by an entire squadron of mosquitoes, each one fully equipped with all the appropriate armaments, as determined as any kamikaze pilot to reach its intended target. Caught off guard, I began to beat my body wildly in an attempt to eliminate a few of the marauders. The mosquitoes accepted that as a challenge, emboldened no doubt by the fact that they were two hundred million in number, and I, a mere mortal, was equipped only with two scrawny hands, both of which spent most of their owner's energy flapping harmlessly in the air.

"What kind of a place is this anyway?" I yelled, as I replaced gratitude with anger and began rummaging through the truck looking for some mosquito spray. "These guys are vicious."

It wasn't long before it dawned on me that I didn't have any mosquito spray, that I was an environmentalist and didn't even believe in the stuff! But I wanted to believe, I can tell you that. In fact, at that moment, what I wanted to do was spray the entire state of Arkansas with mosquito repellent. Being without means,

CHAPTER 1

however, I did the next best thing. I grabbed my sleeping bag, opened the rear door of the van, announced enthusiastically, "We're off," dragged Judy and the cat out of bed, threw all three of us back into the cabin of the truck, and roared once more onto the freeway, putting as much distance as possible between ourselves and Fort Smith. And I didn't stop until the words "vacancy" and "air-conditioned rooms" appeared on the same marquee.

THE WILL OF THE LORD

When I awoke next morning, I wasn't thinking about Fort Smith, strangely enough, but about the ways of the Lord. And the difficulty of knowing whether one is traveling in them. In particular, I was still pondering the wisdom of taking my wife and soon-to-be family clear across the country just so I could go to graduate school. The guilt continued. And so did the doubts.

So far the trip wasn't giving me much comfort. If the Lord was with us, he was being discreet about it. True, he had sent an angel of mercy disguised as Shotgun Sally, but that was about as subtle as they come. Shotgun, moreover, had been our only source of comfort the entire trip. And even that experience turned out to be 90 percent terror and 5 percent wrath, which only left about 5 percent of the encounter in the comfort range. It's hard to get a lot of blessed assurance out of that.

I continued mulling over the Lord's will as we got back into our truck and made our way to a little country kitchen that the motel clerk had recommended for breakfast. It was a few miles from the freeway, but we were tired of fast food and thought it would be chic to sample some of the native cuisine. Within a mile or two of the motel, the road narrowed considerably and began meandering nonchalantly through a sparsely wooded area, full of hills. I was again impressed with the beauty of the landscape and found it hard to keep my eyes on the road.

CHAPTER 1

"Stop the truck, Stan," Judy yelled out. Not having paid much attention to the road, I assumed we were heading for an accident so I slammed on the brakes. Hard. Whatever else one might say about U-Haul trucks, the brakes are excellent. And within seconds our truck had come to a screeching halt, and Judy, Talcott, and I were licking dust off the front window.

"What is it, Honey?" I asked.

"Over there, Stan. Look up on the side of that hill."

I peered out the window, expecting to see a flying saucer or the president of the United States or both. What I saw instead was a small but perfectly average-looking cemetery nestled among the trees about halfway up the hill.

"This is amazing, Judy! It's a cemetery! How could I have lived if I had missed this spectacle? In fact, this is worth dying for, don't you think? Let's get out of the truck and erect a monument to this moment. We'll call it, 'The Moment We Almost Killed Ourselves to Look at a Cemetery' monument. And all of history will be changed because of this experience. Our children will make a pilgrimage here annually, just so they can remember—"

"Stan," Judy interrupted, having gotten used to my sarcasm before 9:00 A.M. and knowing not to take it personally. "You're missing something. Look about a hundred yards to the right of the cemetery, a little further up the hill."

At first I couldn't see what she was talking about. But as I kept looking, I noticed movement a short distance from the cemetery. As I continued scanning to the right, the full picture began to take shape. Beside the well-kept cemetery there was another graveyard, not nearly as beautiful as the first, and not nearly as well maintained. The graves were marked by stones standing in irreverent postures and the grasses beside them were straggly and unmowed. Winding up the hill to the unkept cemetery was a small dirt path, and striding slowly within its borders was an old man, cane in one hand and flowers in the other. He was very feeble. Very determined. And very black.

We watched, spellbound, as the man continued up the trail

and reached an unmarked plot of grass. He stood there quietly, bowed his head, and then suddenly dropped to his knees. The drop was quick and startling, and it made us aware of our own obtrusive involvement in the scene. The man had come to spend time with a loved one and his God, not with two Californians in a U-Haul truck. And he deserved more from us than staring eyes and inquisitive minds. He deserved our absence.

I put the truck in first gear and carefully began to pick up speed. The truck seemed noisier than normal, perhaps because we were trying for silence, perhaps because we were silent ourselves. Judy was the first to disturb the peace.

"What have we done," she asked, ". . . and why?" Her voice was quivering, weak and strong and wondering all at the same time. I knew from the tone that she was talking about history, not the noise of our truck. It wasn't a question as much as a statement. And I wasn't sure she wanted an answer. But I wasn't sure of her logic either. So I decided to throw it back in her lap.

"Why do you say 'we,' Hon? We didn't build that cemetery. It wasn't our ancestors who separated blacks from whites. I'm not sure I want to take responsibility for that. At least, not this morning. I'm having a hard enough time taking responsibility for this trip. I can't take on the sins of America too."

"You know what I mean, Stan," she said gently. "I'm not talking about that cemetery. Or the sins of America. I'm not even talking about whites and blacks. I'm talking about people. Human beings. Why do we treat each other so badly?"

I thought I knew what she was driving at, but I also thought her question overlooked some important details. I was a sociologist, after all, and it seemed to me quite wrong to blame the racial problem in America on humans in general. It was the Europeans who came to the New World, displacing Native Americans in the process and enslaving Africans along the way. To blame all of humanity for the problem was like blaming an entire family for the criminal acts of a son. It hardly seemed fair.

"I'm not trying to excuse the people who did that," she

continued, pointing back at the cemetery. "But I want to know why they did it . . . and I don't want your sociological explanation, either. I want to know how they could have done it. And especially I want to know how Christian people could have let it happen. I want to know why Christians in my hometown call their brown-skinned neighbors "spicks" and "greasers," rather than neighbors. I want to know why we didn't say boo to that working-class family across the hall from us in Blah City. I want to know why people in our church cheat their employer out of a day's labor or cheat their workers out of a fair wage. I want to know why we Christians do these things when the Bible says— from beginning to end, without qualification or reservation or the slightest hint of ambiguity—that we are to love God and love our neighbor as ourselves. That's pretty direct, isn't it? Pretty clear? So why don't we do it?"

It was stated as a question but, of course, was not. Judy knew the answer as well as I, and there was no reason whatsoever for either of us to say another word. People sin. That's the bottom line. Even people who know better. Even people, like us, who have been schooled on Scripture from day one, who believe in its teaching and believe in its God. Though we believe, we don't always act that way. Though we know, we don't always find it easy to put that knowledge into practice. The problem is not knowing God's will, in other words. The problem is doing it.

And then, suddenly, the lights went on and the bells started ringing. I knew, at last, my lifelong quest to know the Lord's will had come to an end. "The problem is not knowing the Lord's will," I said, "the problem is doing it."

I repeated the phrase, as its meaning began to sink in. "The challenge that God has put before me," I realized, "is not to somehow figure out his will at every turn, but to put into practice the will I know. What the Lord desires of me is to obey his commands, not to discern commands where none exist; to live according to what has been revealed, not to demand revelations for all of life's choices; to obey his Spoken Word, not endlessly to fret over words that have yet to be spoken."

So simple, I thought as we continued down the road. So simple and so obviously right that I began wondering how I could have missed it for so long. How could I have spent endless hours trying to decide between right and right, and ignoring the wrong I was doing all along? Why do I struggle with the Lord's will when it isn't necessary, and why do I fail to put the Lord's will into practice when it's as plain as the nose on my face?

Why? Because doing what is right is difficult. It's costly. I learned that in spades at the Holiday Inn at Fort Smith. I didn't want to turn down that room, artfully offered to me in exchange for a lie. I wanted to sleep. I wanted to get some rest. And saying no to the clerk's offer that night was one of the hardest things I had ever done. But according to what I knew, it was right. It was, in other words, the Lord's will. And I really didn't much like it.

But worrying about whether the Lord wants me to go back east to college—that's the kind of thing I like. Oh, it's no fun to worry, that's for sure; psychologically speaking, dealing with the anxiety of indecision is no fun at all. But it's a lot easier than believing that God will take care of you regardless of what decision you make. That's the tough one. That takes faith. That means living with the unknown. That means living like a believer.

Better yet, worrying all the time about the Lord's will is a great way to cover up the fact that I have a problem, a deeply spiritual problem. Because it turns out that, when push comes to shove, I have a difficult time trusting the Lord. When Jesus says, "Do not worry about tomorrow . . . your Father knows what you need," I don't quite believe he means what he says. And so I run around doing precisely what the pagans do—worrying about what I shall eat and drink and wear—but dressing it up nicely with the language of the Lord's will and assuaging my guilty conscience in the process.

You see, to get out of the "Lord's-will game," you really have to believe that God cares for you as much as he says he does.

CHAPTER 1

You really have to believe that, regardless of what decisions you make, if you make them in good faith, the Lord will not abandon you. That he actually will go with you. That he does, in fact, number the hairs on your head. That he really does care for you and love you every bit as much as he says he does.

But that's hard to believe, isn't it? And so what do we do instead? What do I do instead? I worry about those things that God has told me not to worry about and ignore the clear teachings of Scripture. Instead of doing justice and loving mercy, I plead with the Lord to show me which parking space he wants me to use. Instead of walking humbly with my God—believing in my heart that he is a God who can be waited on and trusted and who is always faithful—I badger him to death with questions about his will, the answers to which I probably wouldn't understand if he told me, and are no doubt none of my business anyway. Instead of loving my neighbor, in other words, I love myself.

We're strange creatures, aren't we? Giving away the freedom God wants us to have, on one hand, and taking liberties that are not ours to take on the other; disobeying God's will when it is known, and searching desperately for it when it is not.

At least, that is the way it has often been with me.

But then one day you're driving along the back roads in a U-Haul truck, trying to figure out God's will for your life. And all at once you are massively confronted with the results of not loving your neighbor spread out before you on the side of a hill. It is a scene you'd like to blame on others but cannot. Because too often you have been the one who has not loved your neighbor. Because too often the sin has been your own.

And so, you do what you should have done long ago: bow your head and ask for forgiveness and for the strength to do the Lord's will when it is clearly set before you and to trust him gratefully when it is not. After which, you shift the truck into second gear, press your foot to the accelerator, and know without a doubt that the Creator of Heaven and Earth—the Sovereign God of history, the Great I Am, the One Who Was, and Is, and forever more Will Be—the Lord, your God, walks with you.

34

CHAPTER 2
DISCOVERING WHAT YOU NEED

A DOG'S LIFE

Dogs have always loved me. When I was in college, a number of dogs regularly found their way onto campus. No one knew how they got there. And except for a greyhound named Bus, I didn't even know their names. But that didn't matter. Whenever they saw me, their tails would start wagging, and they would strategically plant themselves in my vicinity, either in my path as I was walking or on top of my feet if I was stationary. Dogs like me. And on the whole, the feeling is mutual.

On the whole. The fact is, dogs are also a nuisance at times. Though dogs tend to be amicable, they are often friendly to a fault, knocking over lamp shades with their tails and slobbering all over your new wingtips. They are usually loyal, as well, and will defend their master's house to the death. But at the same time, they spend most of their energy defending it against noncombatants: barking at neighbors, attacking relatives, and scaring your pastor half to death. Given that one is only visited by malefactors once or twice in a lifetime—and that a dog's term in office extends for only about a decade—chances are great that your loyal dog will spend 99.9 percent of his time accosting the wrong people.

Being liked by dogs, and liking them in return, is no piece of cake. It comes with a cost. At times you wonder if it's worth it.

It wasn't worth it for my dad.

A DOG'S LIFE

I had the good fortune of growing up with a little Pomeranian named Cookie. When I say little, I don't mean simply that she was small as far as dogs go. I mean she was small for a Pomeranian. So we're talking basic diminutive here. I had a habit of acquiring runts, and Cookie was par for the course. Still, she was a purebred, immensely friendly, smart, and astoundingly beautiful when groomed, which wasn't often since we lived on a farm and Cookie had the run of the place. The bottom line, then, was that we had a dog that looked good on paper but spent most of her time looking like a dirty little runt in real life. And I loved her.

My father did not. Not because he had anything against Cookie per se; he just didn't have any use for dogs in general. And "use" was a high value to my dad. Things needed a purpose. A reason for being. And the reasons my dad had in mind related primarily to putting a roof over your head, serving the needy, and living in obedience to God. As far as my dad could tell, a dog didn't help you accomplish any of those things. Thus, a dog wasn't necessary. So why have one?

God, however, having a sense of humor, gave my dad children who loved dogs. And children were definitely part of my dad's reason for being. Though he didn't personally see the value in dogs, his children did; so he was willing to put up with their presence in the house. Which he did on several occasions, the most significant of those being Cookie.

One other thing you should know about my father is that he was not fond of slime. Had someone issued invitations to a mud-pie party, my father would have been the last to arrive. Indeed, he wouldn't have arrived at all. Dirt, grease, and grunge were not something one enjoyed; they were the Enemy, to be avoided at all costs. Again, one has to assume a divine sense of humor because my dad wound up becoming a farmer. And if farming is anything, it is dirt, grease, and grunge. I've long suspected that one reason my dad succeeded fairly quickly at farming is because he was in a mad rush to put distance between himself and the grime. He needed employees. Pronto.

Cookie lived to a fairly ripe old age, which means that she and my dad put up with each other for a good spell. Actually, Cookie didn't put up with anything. She loved my dad as she did nearly everyone else in the world. My dad, on the other hand, smiled politely at Cookie but rarely took his hands out of his pockets or made any effort to bring his hands even close to the dog. The best he could do was to stand at attention—all six-foot-three inches of him, a seeming giant compared to this runt Pomeranian—and smile, while Cookie would look up at him, tail wagging to beat the band and eyes sparkling, wondering whether this would be the day she finally felt my father's touch.

Well that day eventually came, not because my dad was overcome by the wiles of doggiedom, but by the pure essence of slime. One lamentable quality of Pomeranians is that they have long hair nearly everywhere. Everywhere! Long hair is nice in its place—beautiful, in fact—but not when it is located in the vicinity of the tail. It's especially not nice when it comes into contact with less than fully processed intestinal material. In part, this is because hair performs a certain holding action, not allowing all the material to be deposited properly. But it is also problematic because hair tends to commingle with the material, harden, and over time become as solid as a brick. It doesn't fall off, in other words, but becomes a permanent fixture on the dog. It ain't pretty, either.

As Cookie matured and her hair grew, we began to notice the brick problem. It was a problem unencumbered by her grooming habits and totally impervious to our own (actually, we didn't bathe her all that often anyway; a bath for a farm dog is about as effective as a mudpack on a fish). This means, of course, that regardless of what we did, the problem only seemed to evolve. And it was this evolutionary quality that bothered my dad the most. It bothered all of us, to be sure, but it made my dad sick. If Cookie was walking in the opposite direction, Dad either had to avert his eyes or run to the bathroom. He had no other options.

A DOG'S LIFE

Well, all of this came to a head one day as I was arriving home from school. When I jumped out of the bus and ran into our front yard, I noticed Dad over by the barn, standing behind his pickup. I couldn't tell what he was doing, but I made a habit of sticking my nose into Dad's business whenever possible, so I ran straight toward him. When I arrived, I discovered that this was a business I didn't want my nose anywhere near. For there, standing behind the pickup, was my dad—the great slime hater of all time—holding Cookie's tail with his left hand and applying an electric hair clippers with his right, shaving the brickwork off of the dog's backside, while Cookie, absolutely in glory, stood at attention on the bed of the truck. It was a moment like none other in history. A moment that will live in infamy, from my dad's perspective. But a moment of pure delight for his son.

A moment, I might add, distinguished by its incredible brevity. Dad moved those clippers faster than any barber I have ever seen. And within a few seconds the dog was off the pickup and my dad was hustling to the bathroom. But the moment will last forever in my mind's eye. And in my heart.

Dogs are needy. Unlike cats, who can survive jolly well without you, dogs really aren't good at taking care of themselves. They need others to help them out. Other dogs in the wild. Or if domesticated, they need human beings. They need others to help them find food, to scratch their backs, to help them clean their backsides.

And helping is not always something one wants to do. It's not too big an effort to feed them in the morning, if you can afford the food. And even the smallest child finds it easy to give a dog a back scratch, especially when the act is so obviously appreciated. But some of their needs are less pleasant. And then having a needy pet isn't quite so much fun. Nor is being needed. In fact, you wonder if it's really worth it. Why bother, after all? It's hard enough to just take care of yourself. Why take care of a dog as well?

CHAPTER 2

For me the answer came during the summer of 1966. By then, Cookie was almost thirteen years old, and I was between my sophomore and junior years in college. Cookie remained quite active. And we were still pretty close. But most of the year I was away at college so we couldn't really spend much time together. I felt guilty about that, actually. And like parents everywhere, who spend most of their waking hours at work rather than with their children, I tried to convince myself that though our contact was minimal the times together were that much more special. "Quality time" is the euphemism. And I was really into quality time that summer.

Toward the end of the summer, I was involved in a serious automobile accident, and that changed our relationship significantly. The accident left me badly scarred, both in mind and body. Psychologically, I had to deal with the fact that my passenger—my cousin, Paul—was killed. As the driver, I felt responsible, and the weight of that responsibility was heavy. Physiologically, my wounds were burdensome as well. I spent most of the year following the accident entombed in a body cast, confined to my bed.

It's hard to describe what forced confinement does to the human spirit—the key word being *forced*. We all choose confinement at various times in our lives, and we're usually happy to find it. It is wonderful to slip under the covers on a crisp October night. It's a joy to batten down the hatches in winter and snuggle up in front of the fire with a good book. And it's a relief beyond description to find the bathroom vacant and know the satisfaction of closed doors and lavatorious solitude.

But when the confinement is obligatory, the picture changes. Instantly, the world from which you once sought refuge is now beyond your grasp. You wake up in the morning and you can't roll out of bed. You finish reading a chapter of a book and you can't stand up for a stretch. You accomplish your bathroom duties and you can't flush or escape the residue of your own pollution.

You're stuck. Stuck with your bed. Stuck with your position. Stuck with yourself.

The problem is multiplied tenfold by the fact that you can't seek out others either. Until you are confined, you don't realize the extent to which life is made up of a fragile web of relationships. Who you are is all wrapped up with those on whom you depend. Humans need to feel connected. When you're immobilized, however, you lose the option of making connections. You have to wait on the whimsical overtures of others— others who are busy, who have their own lives to lead, and who have no practical reason to make connections with you. In the end, whether alone or not, you feel vulnerable to loneliness. And often you are.

Many people did yeoman's service during the summer of 1966 to make me feel less vulnerable. My mother, especially, will go down in the Good Samaritans' Hall of Fame for her efforts on my behalf. For seven months, she essentially made me her career. I remember, too, many friends and relatives who spliced me into their schedules, regularly stopping by the house just to remind me that they were still a part of my world. And finally, I'll never forget my two-year-old niece, Cheryl, who for some inexplicable reason seemed to find pleasure in simply sitting on the edge of my bed, keeping me company. Her pleasure was incomprehensible to me. And for that reason, she was a wellspring of comfort and joy.

But eventually, all these good folk were required to leave. They had work to do, places to go, people to see. And every time they departed, I was not only reminded of their love, but also of the precarious nature of their affections. To receive their love, you see, I was totally dependent on their good will. I could give them nothing in exchange, nothing that they needed or desired. I could only wait for their return, hoping that in a day or two they would still want to be a part of my world, hoping that they would still want to give of themselves to someone who had nothing to offer.

Except—except for this little runt Pomeranian named Cookie. Who did not leave my side. Who had nowhere else to go. And who—and this was the best part—still needed me. True, I could no longer feed her. Nor throw her around on the floor. Nor scare the daylights out of her when she came running around the corner of the house. But none of that really mattered. Because I could still reach down from my bed and give her nose a little tweak. And that was enough to send her tail into paroxysms of unmitigated joy. I could do something for her.

Of course, if truth be known, I needed her more than she needed me. I guess you could say that I needed to be needed. But she did a lot more for me than that. Most importantly, she exuded energy, bouncing off of walls she couldn't negotiate, and acting like a rampant lion each time she spotted a frog on the other side of the window. Her exuberance was in marked contrast to some visitors, I might add, who oiled their way around my bed and spoke in hushed tones of ethereal reverence. I'm sure they were just trying to do the right thing. But they reminded me of death, not life, and their presence was something less than comforting.

But Cookie was always a comfort. She was my persistent link to the fullness of life, to the God who was our Creator. And by her presence, and the things of which she reminded me, she reinvigorated my soul.

A DOG GONE

"Hey, Stan," Biff yelled as we shot out of class. "Let's go over to the mail room before lunch."

Biff was always heading for the mail room. No one blamed him. Between the money his parents sent him and the steamy letters he received from his girlfriend, Wendy, Biff had lots of reasons to check his mail. And few of us minded going with him. A mere whiff of one of Wendy's letters was enough to send any young lad's imagination soaring.

"Sure, why not," I responded, though I knew my own mailbox would be empty. Mom had written just the day before, and I had terminated all off-campus liaisons since I met Judy. Nevertheless, one of Wendy's letters made it worth the hike up to the mail room. "Let's check it out."

It was the fall of 1967, and after a year's convalescence from the accident, I was back amidst ivy, none the worse for wear, beginning my junior year of college. I was enjoying college life as never before, partly because of my newfound relationship with Judy, but also because I had finally been released from the prison of my body cast. Every opportunity seemed like a privilege now, and I found great joy in just walking around campus and even going to class. Life as a student was grand.

There was one exception to this serenity, and his name was Blotto. I can't really remember his name, nor whether he was a he or a she or an it. Blotto, however, pretty much brings the right picture to mind, and I can't imagine a female acting the way he did, so I think we'll stick with the masculine gender for the time being. I suppose you've guessed by now, Blotto was a dog.

A big dog. With lips that drooped to his knees and saliva that cascaded the rest of the way to the ground. This meant Blotto's mouth made constant contact with the earth, except on those occasions when the wind was strong enough to break the saliva connection and send the gooey stuff flying in one direction or the other. People avoided Blotto on windy days.

To be honest, people avoided Blotto every day, though that was not easily accomplished. He had a keen eye and could spot you coming a mile away. He also had a good nose and could smell newly polished shoes anywhere on campus. This was important to Blotto since his primary mission in life was to bring his saliva into contact with shiny shoes. He seemed to find freshly pressed pants satisfying as well, and a combination of the two absolutely made his day. On Sunday mornings Blotto was in heaven.

It will come as no surprise, then, that Blotto loved me. All dogs love me, but I was extra special as far as Blotto was concerned. I'm not sure if this was because I tended to keep my penny loafers polished or just because of my winsome personality, but Blotto was absolutely ga-ga over me. I could be in a crowd of thousands coming out of the gymnasium and Blotto would pick me out. It was uncanny. And when Blotto headed my way, everyone else was more than willing to let him pass by—Blotto going through a crowd was akin to Moses parting the Red Sea.

So as Biff and I headed for the mail room I had a suspicion that Blotto was on my trail. I had just gotten my pants back from the cleaners, and my loafers were brand-new, so it seemed like an opportunity Blotto couldn't miss. To avoid El Saliva, then, I asked Biff if we could walk through the administration building on our way to the mail room—an absolutely Blotto-proof building from my experience. (I think it had something to do with the fact that trustee meetings were held there; if Blotto ever invaded a meeting

meeting of the trustees, the college would have had to have gone into receivership just to pay the cleaning bills.)

We made it into the administration building and walked to the building's back exit. It was only a short jaunt from there up to the mail room, so I was starting to become a bit more optimistic. I opened the door, stuck my head out, and looked in every conceivable direction—including the trees (I know dogs can't climb trees but if Blotto ever figured it out, I knew I was in trouble)—and made a dash toward the mail room.

To my amazement, Blotto was nowhere in sight. I was so surprised by his nonpresence, in fact, that when I got to the top of the hill, I slowed down so I could scan the area more carefully. *Blotto must be around here someplace,* I thought. As I stopped in front of the mail room door, I took one more long look at the campus below. Again, I was struck by the beauty of the environs, from the green shrubs at my feet, to the trees around the buildings, to the Pacific Ocean far in the distance. It was a spectacular scene. But most amazing of all was the fact that Blotto was not a part of it. Where in the world had the big lug gone?

My answer came in a bound when I opened the mail room door. The minute I opened it, Blotto the Magnificent hurled himself against my body, his lugubrious lips landing first on my chest and then slithering in slow motion down my shirt, past my pants and eventually coming to rest on my brand-new shoes. The shoes were his objective; when he finally arrived there, he suddenly froze, his lips draped comfortably over them, his tail sticking high in the air, waving to all of his fans in the mail room.

And oh what happy fans they be! Happy that Blotto had turned his affections to someone else. Happy that it had been me. Happy simply to have witnessed anew the triumph of Blottodom over mankind.

"Get out of here, you dumb palooka!" I said as I tried to extricate my feet from under his mouth by giving a swift kick upward. The kick must have packed more of a wallop than I had intended, because Blotto's head went flying backward, his lips acting like rubber bands, stretching to their maximum potential, and then spring-loading saliva all over the mail room. The scene would have been humorous—with all of Blotto's former fans now heading for cover—except that the dog went tumbling across the room, winding up in a corner, and then just cowered there as if he expected another blow.

I hadn't thought the kick had been that vicious, and for a moment I started to feel sorry for the guy. But after a moment's reflection, it dawned on me that Blotto got what he deserved. That opinion was reinforced, I should add, when I looked down at my clothes and assessed the damage. I decided to tough it out.

"That's good," I said sternly, pointing at Blotto. "That's a good place for you. You stay there."

For the first time in his life, Blotto responded obediently. I mean, he didn't even make a move. He just sat there, breathing heavily, pinning me with his eyes. I couldn't tell whether he was coping with feelings of rejection (it had never occurred to me that he was capable of such emotions) or just getting ready to pounce on me again. But at least he was inert for a change. And that seemed like an improvement, all things considered. I decided to get my mail.

As I walked over to my mailbox, it was evident to everyone in the room that Biff's expedition had met with grand success. The mail room smelled like the perfumery at I. Magnan's. And sure enough, when I found Biff, he was sitting on a bench in the middle of the room, reading a letter with a stupid smile on his face. Obviously, Biff had struck a rich vein.

When I looked in my mailbox, I was surprised to see that I had received a letter as well, though it certainly wasn't up to Biff's standards. It smelled like paper, for one thing, but it was also relatively thin (Biff always got ten pagers—his girlfriend used incredibly big letters for effect). I retrieved my letter and noticed that it was from Mom. *Odd,* I thought. *I just got something from her yesterday. I wonder what's up?* As I opened the letter, I made my way over to Biff's bench and took a seat beside him.

"Dear Stan," my mom began, "I know I just wrote to you

yesterday, but I thought you'd want to know that Cookie died last night. She was having problems walking and so we . . ."

I continued reading, though the task became progressively more difficult as my eyes moistened and the letter's first sentence began to sink in. I proceeded—trying to do the manly thing—until I realized that something other than my eyes was starting to get wet. Blotto was back, and this time he had his muzzle (including lips) on my lap. It was an incredibly stupid move, given what had just happened, and he accomplished it with a degree of stealth I hadn't imagined possible.

"Get out of here," Biff broke in, pushing at Blotto's rear end with his foot. "Leave the guy alone, will ya. . . ."

"No, Biff!" I yelled out quickly, as I pushed Biff's foot away with my own. "Let him be. It's okay. It's . . . it's okay." Biff was stunned by the move, and I could tell that he didn't know whether to kick me back or return to his reading material.

Before he could decide, I held Mom's letter in the air and gave him the news. "My dog died, Biff," I said, as I finally powered up enough to use my voice. "You know, Cookie? The runt Pomeranian I was telling you about? The one with the brick work on her rear end? Well . . . well, she's gone."

My left hand was on Blotto's head, moving involuntarily, fingers scratching in ways that only a dog could love. Or understand.

"She was over thirteen years old," I continued, after a few more deep breaths. "Pretty old, for a dog, I guess. But not old enough for me, Biff. Not nearly old enough for me. . . ."

We sat there in silence for a few moments, Biff now with his letter in his lap, and I with Blotto in mine.

Biff broke the silence. "Stan? I know Cookie didn't live long enough, as far as you're concerned. But . . . well, I was thinking. You've mentioned a hundred times what a great companion Cookie was after your accident. And, well, she did live long enough to see you through that. That's kinda neat, you know?"

I pulled my body forward so I could grab onto Blotto with both hands. "Yeah," I said, as I buried my fingers in his hair. "Kinda neat."

GONE TO THE DOGS

It seems to me that with every dog, there ought to come—as standard equipment—a little tag that reads: "Warning: This animal will be a pain in the neck . . . until needed."

There are those who find the dog-owning experience a joy from beginning to end. They are the patient, nurturing types, who relish the whole blooming training process and who count every accident or indiscretion as an opportunity for growth and learning. But for the rest of us, who have regular jobs and regular dispositions and plenty of headaches as it is, the dog-owning business is a chore about 90 percent of the time (except during the first year of the dog's life, when the percentage is much, much higher). Dogs are needy creatures. And in their neediness, they're a burden.

It strikes me, however, that human beings could come with the same warning tag. Because people are a lot like dogs. In fact, though we humans don't like to admit it, one of the things that distinguishes us from most animals is that we are a lot more needy than they are. This is obvious to anyone who has been a parent as well as a pet owner. If you're a parent, you know that for the first few years of your baby's life, you had to do almost everything for your child. Feeding, clothing, protection from the elements—all these things had to be accomplished by you. Had you let your baby alone for even a day or two, chances are your baby wouldn't have survived.

GONE TO THE DOGS

Now, think of what happens when your cat has kittens. What does the mother do? Well, she gives them a little cleaning, nudges them toward the soda fountain, and that's about it. After that, they're off, finding their own way to the snack bar, teaching themselves how to run and fight and fend off enemies. They may periodically munch on a mouse their mother brings home for a treat, and she may have to protect them from the Old Man periodically, but on the whole, they're on their own. And they'll be almost totally on their own in a few months.

The problem with humans is that we're not constructed with as many built-in instructions as most other animals. The cat does not require a great deal of training because it is born with an internal guidance system. Given a modest amount of education and the right environment, the cat will do catlike things. People, on the other hand, accomplish peoplelike tasks only after a great deal of instruction. It takes years and years of training to simply become a normal human being. And it takes a lifetime of discipline and encouragement to become really good at it.

Now this is not to offer an overly simplistic lesson on human behavior, but to make a point: By any measure, we humans are extraordinarily needy creatures. The strongest among us are needy when compared to the vast majority of species. And that neediness is the result of who we are, not any failing on our part. By constitution, in other words, we are highly dependent upon one another. We cannot simply receive a little training and then go off and live productive lives. To be fully human, a great number of other people have to pour themselves into us, giving of themselves to turn us into reputable folk.

None of this is an accident, by the way. Or a freak of nature. The Bible makes clear that we were created as needy creatures right from the start. One of the most remarkable things about the Genesis story is that it makes our neediness a central fact of our creation. If you reread those chapters, you will discover that not much is said about the peculiarities of God's special creation, aside from the fact that they *are* special and that they have a unique set of responsibilities and obligations. But there is one thing about Adam that is stated flat out and without equivocation: "It is not good for the man to be alone." God created humans to need one another. Solitude is neither good for us nor a part of God's original plan.

In spite of the way sin has come to pervert God's creation, we can see the consequences of God's design all around us. We see it in the helplessness of every newborn child. We see it in the midst of every friendship and family bond. We see it at every wedding, at every party, at every event where human beings come together to share their joy and merriment. We see it at every funeral, at every tragedy, at every event where human beings come together to share one another's grief, to keep the downhearted from losing heart. We need one another for much more than procreation. We need one another to be human, to fulfill the intentions of our Creator.

So why, then, do we sometimes act more like cats than dogs? Why do we sometimes strut through life as if we hadn't a care in the world? Why do we find such glory in individual achievement and act as if our accomplishments are purely our own? And far more tragic than any of this, how can we look the needy in the face and ignore their needs? If we are needy by virtue of how God created us, then don't we know the importance of being needed and meeting the needs of others in return? And finally—coming back to the subject of canines and making the question more personal at the same time—how could I give a needy creature like Blotto a swift kick across the room just for trying to shower me with affection?

At one level the answer to these questions is as complicated as human beings themselves. It would exhaust all the resources of the social sciences and traditional wisdom combined even to scratch the surface. But at another, more fundamental level the answer is not complicated at all: We avoid the needy, not in spite of our own neediness, but because of it. Or to put it more accurately, it is because our needs have not been met that we find it difficult to meet the needs of others.

GONE TO THE DOGS

The problem is sin and what it has done to the human condition. God created us as needy beings and gave us himself and one another to meet that need. Sin, however, separated us from the fullness of those relationships and left us stranded with our needs unmet. We are, in a very real sense, unfulfilled creatures, starved for a wholeness we do not have, yearning to be complete. It is a hunger that can only be satisfied by the One who created us in the first place, and yet that is not the way we normally choose to handle it. Such an approach requires facing up to our sin, for one thing, and repentance is a messy business to say the least. But it necessitates a daily regimen of self-sacrifice, for another—taking up one's cross, as Jesus put it, and laying up treasures where they will do you some good.

The alternative—even for those who know better, like me—is to attempt to satisfy the need on your own. We are rather creative in these attempts and there is no end to the number of ways one can go about it. Sometimes we invest ourselves in a job, hoping that work will bring us fulfillment. Sometimes we try to find our satisfaction in things or highs or goals. Sometimes we attempt to manipulate others into liking us, by buying them off or impressing them with our wealth or knowledge or beauty, assuming that their adoration will bring us satisfaction. And sometimes we simply deny that we have such needs, declaring ourselves islands and pretending to live that way.

How we go about it really doesn't matter, though, because the effect is the same. Either we so desperately try to satisfy our own needs that we don't have time to notice that others need us, or, having convinced ourselves of our own needlessness, we resent the neediness of others (reminding us, as they do, that we are living a lie). In the end, the result is the same. A lot of needy people running around, acting like cats, ignoring the simple fact that others need them too. Ignoring, that is, how we were created. And why.

Until one day, you find yourself so preoccupied with your new shoes that you're willing to give an affectionate dog a swift

CHAPTER 2

kick just for slobbering on them. You don't think much about it at the time, except that he had it coming, until you learn that you just lost the one who took care of you during your time of need. And then it finally dawns on you that you too have been a slobbering fool at times in your life—as a helpless infant, an awkward teenager, and a recuperating accident victim—and yet there were those who gave of themselves to meet your needs, nevertheless. When you were weak, they were strong. When you were down, they didn't kick you out.

And in the humility that only repentance brings, you give yourself to the one who is needy, burying your hands in the needs of another, only to find that it is the needy who finally give you the comfort you seek.

CHAPTER 3
DISCOVERING YOUR SELF

A SELF POSSESSED

Upon arriving someplace new, one of your initial objectives is to avoid making a fool of yourself. That is probably the case regardless of where you go. But it is especially true if your destination is a prominent university. I say that for two reasons. First, the primary commodity at a university is knowledge. And where smarts is the product, stupidity is to be avoided at all costs. Secondly, though a few people manage to make lucrative careers at a university, money is rarely the motive of the academic. The prize at the university isn't gold, it's prestige. And the scholar of high repute is anything but a fool.

When we arrived at Preppie University, therefore, we had a number of objectives in mind—securing a reasonably priced apartment, getting Judy plugged into her new kindergarten job, getting me started in my courses, finding a community of believers to worship with, that sort of thing—but the primary goal was to look halfway intelligent.

Well, you can imagine the difficulty of the task. People who drive along the freeway, talking to their wives with their heads sticking out the window, are not normally assumed to be paragons of high culture or intellectual refinement. It was clear we had our work cut out for us.

Nevertheless, as surprising as it may seem, things went amazingly well during the first few months of our stay. Judy, especially, managed the task expertly. She taught in a rural school system about twenty miles outside of the city, and she was the first kindergarten teacher in the history of the school. As a result, her presence was taken as evidence of "progress," by school administrators and parents alike, and she was the recipient of a good deal of attention and adulation. Having been trained as a kindergarten teacher, she was the resident guru in an experiment everyone wanted to succeed. Whatever Judy wanted, Judy got—including a classroom the size of Texas, with a piano, kitchen, and private bath to boot. No doubt about it: Judy was a knockout in the first-impression department.

And all things considered (that is, given the possibilities), I didn't do too badly myself. Without embarrassment, I was able to sign up for the right courses, secure a study carrel in the library, meet with my advisor, and make two or three friends among the ranks of fellow graduate students. Granted, these were not difficult tasks. But I fancied I carried them off with a certain degree of aplomb.

For example, when my advisor told me—"You realize, don't you, that the fact that you already have a master's degree from Blah University won't count for much around here; we basically look at you like any other first-year student; you've got the same hurdles to overcome, and you'll have to prove yourself in this environment just like everybody else"—I responded with a confident, "You bet." When I walked out of his office, of course, I passed out in the middle of the hall. But I thought I had handled the bad news fairly well, considering the fact that my advisor had just informed me that the totality of my previous two years' experience, including five qualifying exams and a legion of research papers, had been a complete waste of time.

Within a month or so, however, I learned that my advisor was not nearly as fearsome as I had initially imagined. He did have high expectations, that was clear, but he was also genuinely interested in me and my academic progress. Over time, moreover, his interest began to grow. That was due in part to the fact that I was taking a course from him and he seemed to like my work. But it was also fueled by our mutual academic interests. When he discovered that I was planning to specialize in stratification and religion, he became noticeably more outgoing, stopping me in the halls just to chat and asking questions about my wife and our adjustment to the area.

Eventually, the big moment came—that day when you finally realize you are part of a professor's inner circle, when the fog lifts, the sun breaks through, and you know without doubt that you're on the fast track toward doctordom: My advisor invited Judy and me over to his home for an evening of dinner and conversation. Not under obligation from the department chairperson, mind you. And not as part of a large group of graduate students either. Oh no. This was an evening just for us. Because I was a special student. Because I was worth opening up his home to. Because I had arrived.

Well, we showed up at his home in our sixties best, which out of decency I won't describe in any detail but for which we would have been thrown out on our ears in any reputable society, before or since. Suffice it to say, we thought we looked chic. Judy, at this point, was in her fifth month of pregnancy and was, thus, starting to blossom. In any other era that would have meant distinctive clothing, designed specifically for such maternal conditions. In the sixties, however, it meant absolutely nothing whatsoever. Everyone and everything looked maternal, regardless of whether it was designed for male or female, beauty or beast.

That was a problem for women who wanted to look pregnant, by the way, since they found it hard to announce their condition visually. It was a problem for husbands, as well, since many of them were rather proud about the part they played in their wives' condition and yet felt cheated out of their due respect. But I think it was especially unfair to the rest of the world since it put everyone else in the position of having to guess whether or not someone was expecting. And all things considered, there is probably no question on earth more risky than, "Excuse me, would you happen to be pregnant?" Many friendships have ended with that question, and not a few diets have commenced.

Nevertheless, I thought there was no doubting that Judy was pregnant, not because of her clothing but because of her look. I have heard it said that expectant mothers have a special glow, and before Judy's pregnancy I had always assumed that was pure folklore. Not so. She looked radiant from head to toe. Now, I know you're thinking that this is a biased statement, coming as it does from her husband. But I wasn't the only one who noticed it. In conversation after conversation, I discovered that people would confirm my analysis.

"Excuse me, sir. I'm sorry to bother you, seeing that you're in a hurry to finish your Christmas shopping. But my wife is pregnant, and, well, don't you think she looks absolutely luminescent?"

"What? Oh. Uh . . . oh, yeah. She looks, uh, wonderful. Just . . . wonderful."

In the entirety of Judy's pregnancy, not one person ever tried to refute my claim. Not one. That's astounding, actually, when you think about it. Statistically, it certainly merits attention. Social scientists assume they're doing well when they get a majority of people to agree on anything. But, here, in my survey, I had 100 percent agreement. So I knew that I was dealing with scientific fact.

The point of all this is simply that, in spite of what we were wearing on the night of our visit to my advisor's house, it was apparent that Judy was pregnant and I was not. This was a good thing since, even in the sixties, pregnant husbands were looked down on. That may come as a surprise, given the general fascination with all things fecund. But those were the days of natural foods and natural childbirth, and pregnant husbands were anything but natural. Of course, men were allowed—and even encouraged—to participate fully in the baby-having process. And in some cases, it didn't seem to matter who the man was nor what

CHAPTER 3

part he chose to play. But most people drew the line with childbearing. Husbands were not supposed to have the baby itself.

More importantly, however, as far as that evening was concerned, Judy's pregnancy was a great conversation piece, and it immediately gave us something to talk about. My advisor and his wife were fairly young and had not yet started a family of their own. But they were working on it and, for that reason, extremely interested in all the particulars. They wanted to know how Judy was feeling ("Great"), when the baby was due ("February"), why we had decided to have a baby at this time in our lives ("It just seemed right")—the whole nine yards. Of course, we lied about everything except the baby's due date—and that turned out to be erroneous as well—but the circumstances seemed to nearly preclude the possibility of truth.

Judy almost always tells people that she's feeling great, regardless of how she's really feeling. This is not because she's a liar but because most of the time she is feeling great (the doctor says she has a high pain threshold and I believe it; she's always the last one to notice hunger pains, especially when it's her turn to do the cooking). What this means is that, even when she isn't in top form, as during the first few months of her pregnancy, it doesn't change her overall estimate of her condition. On the whole, she's feeling good. So why burden people with the minor fact that she turns green every other morning?

As far as the question about the timing of the pregnancy is concerned, I must confess to being the culprit there. Judy would have gladly said, "Oh, it was a mistake," and told them the whole story of our experience in that seedy little motel room in San Jose. But you have to keep in mind who I was and to whom we were talking. I was a budding sociologist, remember? And sociologists are supposed to know something about human beings, especially human beings in groups and relationships. Now, if there is anything central to the whole business of conception, it is a relationship, right? And so I figured I was supposed to know

58

something about it, at least enough to engage in a little family planning.

And then, of course, we were talking to my advisor. This was the man who was going to certify whether I really was a sociologist, after all. He held my professional life in his hands. How was I going to tell him that in this—the most central of relational activities—I hadn't a clue? One could imagine his letter of recommendation on my behalf: ". . . generally, Dr. Gaede is well versed in matters relating to bonding and familial obligations, but in the area of intimacy and procreation, he seems to think with his glands rather than his brains." I know now that I was exaggerating the problem, but it seemed a probable outcome at that point in my life—and an intolerable one, at that. And so, with a great deal more calculation than my wife managed in her response, I shaved the truth. To the point that the truth could not be seen.

Apparently, however, the Lord noticed. And in due time, so did everyone else. The circumstances are still hazy, but as I recall, we were all sitting around the coffee table, sharing appetizers and lies, when my wife suddenly stood up and asked to use the bathroom. That took me by surprise, since I am usually the one in our family that inspects the facilities. Judy, on the other hand, having the threshold advantage, typically manages to wait until we get back to our house. She never just stands up and announces her intentions. So I knew something was up.

My advisor politely pointed to his newly decorated study— which looked more like a library than an office—and told her that the facilities were just through the door. Judy quickly headed in that direction. But the minute she disappeared into his study, we heard a cough, a thump, and a modest moan. When we arrived, Judy was resting comfortably on the floor, as were her semi-digested appetizers and other assorted tidbits. It was an odd scene for at least three reasons.

First, Judy was on the floor. The second odd thing about the

CHAPTER 3

picture was the look on Judy's face. She appeared to be totally at peace. In fact, she looked absolutely serene, as if she were perfectly content with herself and the world around her. Now, the problem here was the contrast between her look and her condition. For one thing, her smile was only inches from her appetizers. And that, in and of itself, seemed rather unconventional. But for another, she had just regurgitated all over my professor's newly decorated study and there seemed to be lots of reasons not to be happy about that. The carpet, Judy's reputation, my sociological future, just to mention a few, all seemed to hang in the balance. And each of them appeared to preclude the possibility of reverie. Nevertheless, there she was: my wife, lying on the floor, happy as a clam, looking like a child on her first visit to Disneyland.

The final strange thing about the picture was its effect on me. After the initial shock of realizing that we had just been exposed as liars and my professor was going to spend the next year or so studying with a mask over his nose—after all that, nothing really seemed to matter except the fact that Judy was okay and we would soon be on our way home. In fact, once Judy regained consciousness and it was clear that she wasn't injured in any way, the primary feeling I had was one of relief. It was almost as though a great weight had been lifted from my shoulders. I had been freed up to run and jump and play and be myself again.

In part, I suppose that the relief came in the realization that Judy wasn't hurt. There is a sudden twist in values that takes place at a time like that, where in one moment your greatest concern is how to keep the pâté from falling off the wafer, and the next you are worried about your wife's life. Even when the event seems to put your credibility and career on the line—as this one seemed to—the contrast between those values and the value of your marriage partner has the effect of slapping you back into reality. "Forget the carpet, dummy," a voice demands, "this is your wife!" And quickly you obey, your priorities restored by the sheer weight of circumstances.

But there was more to the relief than this. Riding home that night, it eventually dawned on me that I had been relieved of more than false values. I had had the burden of false pretense lifted from my shoulders as well. There we were, trying to look so good, attempting to convince our company as well as ourselves of our own importance and immeasurable wisdom, and—boom—all of our humanity spills out on the floor for everyone to see. We were not wonderful, we were sick. We were not perfect, we used the bathroom occasionally and sometimes we missed. We were not smart, we went to people's houses and pretended we were something we were not.

And, so, the cat was out of the bag. What we knew to be true deep down inside, they now understood as well. Our insides had come out. Quite literally. And the sense of relief was immense. Nearly palpable. We could be ourselves. We were finally free.

A SELF DISCLOSED

Of course, we might have had to change careers as well! And that is the downside of the whole "'fessing up" business. There is tremendous relief to exposure. But there is also the risk that people may not like what they see and, as a result, tell you to get out. Or move on. Or find a new major.

Nevertheless, once you've done it, you really don't care. Indeed, the relief is so complete and the feeling is so wonderful that you wonder why you were concerned about the consequences in the first place. It's like the initial time you go skinny-dipping in a pond: the risks are great but the feeling of freedom is too grand to worry about a possible Peeping Tom. Or, in my case, a Peeping Mary.

And that raises the question, why do we worry? Why don't we go skinny-dipping more often—metaphorically speaking, of course? That was an especially popular question in the sixties, when letting it all hang out was next to godliness in popularity. More so, I suspect. "Why do we hide behind so many masks?" we used to ask. "Why do we play roles all the time and act as if we are something we are not? Why can't we just be ourselves, for crying out loud? Why do we always have to fake it?"

Those are particularly hard questions to answer after you have one of those "freedom experiences" such as we had at my advisor's house. The relief is so cathartic that you wonder why you waited so long to get it out. And the likelihood is great that you will kick yourself all the way home for being such a pretender in the first place. And promise yourself about a thousand times that it will never happen again. "I will be myself, Lord; you can bank on it."

But then, in less than twenty-four hours, you are back into the grind, doing what you always did, acting the way you always acted. And wondering how you managed to get up the nerve to be yourself the day before. And on it goes.

I am a good example of the problem, I think. From what I've been told, I was a fairly outgoing child. I was constantly playing with friends and constantly ignoring all those responsibilities of a more solitary nature, such as practicing my saxophone or doing my homework. Still, I don't recall ever thinking of myself as being particularly sociable. What I remember, instead, is a young boy trying to earn the esteem of his peers and often failing. I don't mean that I considered myself a failure; for some reason, I always had a measure of self-confidence. Nevertheless, peer approval did not come easily for me. It was a battle.

And a battle I was determined to win. During puberty and my teenage years, I worked hard at gaining the admiration of others, and given my station in life and the town and culture within which I lived, that meant one of three things. First, I could become a good athlete. Second, I could become a social whiz-kid, an entertainer. And third, I could simply become "cool." Any one of these attributes was sure to gain peer approval, but a combination was absolute dynamite.

Now, believe it or not, in my early years, I actually thought I had a shot at achieving some recognition in all three of these areas. I realize that this will come as a shock, given what you know of me, but the dreams of a young man are undeterred by reality. And I had dreams of becoming a fabulous basketball player, whose every utterance was studded with wit and charm, and whose persona was just as smooth as silk.

CHAPTER 3

The first real blow to this ambition came during my freshman year in high school when I was cut from the C team after only a few days of basketball practice. Now, you have to keep in mind that C is two down from A, and that the A team was the one with all the quality players on it. So getting dropped from the C team was not like being declared a non-star. It was more like being told you were a basketball bozo and had no business being anywhere in the vicinity of the gymnasium. Unfortunately, I was told that again when I tried out for the C team during my sophomore year. So I had to face the facts. Larry Bird I was not.

That still left me with two options in my quest for peer approval: I could become the life of the party, and/or I could perfect the art of being cool. Now, the first option was one I often dreamed of but knew was really beyond my grasp. In the bathtub or standing under a shower, I could be witty and humorous beyond belief. Jokes there brought tears to my eyes. But when I was in the midst of real people rather than water, at a real social gathering, my tongue nearly always failed me. At most, I could interject a pithy sentence or two. But I was absolutely incapable of holding forth for any length of time. Bill Cosby I was not.

Which left me with being cool. Again, I know this seems like an unlikely path given what you already know about me. People who drive down the road with their heads out the window are not only less than cultured, they are completely off the edge of the cool continuum. Nevertheless, you must keep in mind that I would not have done something that ludicrous as a teenager. Moreover, though my tongue didn't work with the dexterity I desired, the rest of me moved pretty well. I was not ugly. I had a head of hair that could accommodate itself to the changing demands of pop culture. And I fancied that my gait was well composed, that I could saunter with the best of them. So, even if Bird or Cosby were beyond my reach, maybe I could be a Redford?

So I put all my energies into being cool. Everything I did had to be examined and perfected, from the way I dressed, to the way I talked, to the way I walked, to the way I sat—everything. I remember practicing how to wave to someone while driving. I decided the best approach was to give a short, crisp salute just beneath the window visor. That way, if the other person didn't wave back, you could conclude the salute by pulling the visor down and camouflage your unreciprocated wave. Amazing.

Did it work? Well, I don't know. It certainly didn't work well enough to get me into the circles of the elite. I never was asked to join the Key Club, for example, and BMOC's merely tolerated me. But I managed to have some social success here and there. I dated some wonderful women. Drove some fine cars. And had about as good a time as anyone else in high school. So, yes, I guess it worked.

But it also came at a price. Being cool not only required a great deal of navel gazing, it also forced me to be overly concerned about the judgments of others. And that left me feeling a bit fake. Unreal. Was I being myself or simply trying to live up to the expectations of my peers? Success, in other words, seemed to come at the expense of self-satisfaction. This feeling was, no doubt, reinforced by my faith. Try as I might, I had a hard time convincing myself that God was as interested in my "being cool" as I was. And I doubted that Jesus spent a great deal of time practicing his wave. Even when I was winning the battle of peer approval, within my soul I felt as if I was losing the war.

At the age of nineteen, as I've mentioned, I was involved in a serious car accident. And that event, along with a long period of recuperation, enabled me to reassess my life as well as my priorities. One of the first conclusions I reached was that life was too short to be wasted on playing games and trying to be something I was not. I discovered that the people I genuinely admired were not those who were cool but those who had the gumption to say what they thought and do what they believed to be right.

So, I resolved to change. To be myself. To wave regardless of whether someone else waved back. To admit my faults, regardless of consequences. To say what I thought rather than what I assumed others wanted me to say. To do what I wanted to do rather than what I believed others wanted me to do. In short, I decided to perfect the art of self-disclosure—to become, finally, the fully transparent self I had always assumed I should be.

Of course, I failed. Oh, I suppose there were victories now and then, moments when I got up the courage to say what I really thought, times when I really let my hair down. But those times were not the norm. Nor were they always as satisfying as I had assumed they would be. I especially remember one day when I finally got up the courage to tell a fellow graduate student that his ideas about religion were uninspired—something I had been wanting to tell him for months—and then feeling sort of sick in the aftermath.

On the whole, then, my personality remained relatively unchanged. What did change as a result of the accident, however, was my lifestyle. I gave up some activities I thought weren't right. I selected a new college, with a new set of friends, who helped me live according to my standards. I began to develop career aspirations based more upon my gifts and the needs of others rather than what would bring me pleasure or wealth. But as far as my basic person was concerned—how I presented myself to the world—nothing particularly changed.

And, naturally, I felt deeply guilty. These were the sixties, after all, and we were told we should be ourselves. "Scrape away all the scum of society and be yourself," we used to say. But I just couldn't seem to manage it. Try as I might, I continued to dress and talk and live like my peers. I took their ideas into consideration before talking, and I rarely said anything that was deliberately offensive. All in all, I discovered that being yourself was not an easy ambition.

Nevertheless, I continued to hold up the ideal of self-disclosure—and to feel guilty about it—right through marriage and graduate school. But then an interesting thing happened. We had children. And with children came the opportunity to see the self-disclosure thing in operation, not from the perspective of the idealist, but from the vantage point of a parent. A parent who loved his children. And wanted them to reach the potential their Creator intended.

At first, I assumed this meant that I should encourage my children to be the kind of person I wished I could be: a totally up-front, honest, fully self-disclosing kind of guy. I taught them to say what they felt. To speak their minds, regardless of what others might think of them. Of course, Judy tried to temper that with good manners and courteous behavior. But the emphasis was on self-disclosure. My kids were going to be themselves.

But over time, I began to see what happened to such children. They got creamed. I mean really creamed. Easily manipulated by peers, such children quickly become the butt of jokes and the object of ridicule and derision. Even adults, who often claim to enjoy the fresh naïveté of young people, find straight-shooting children difficult to handle. For them, it indicates a lack of respect and self-control. In short, instead of being admired for their honesty, the self-disclosing child is a fat target for peers and a worry for adults. It hardly seemed like the ideal route to personal growth and development.

Fortunately for my children, when the bombardment came, they quickly discarded the idealism of their father and grabbed the social armor necessary to protect themselves and do battle. And because God is gracious and able to overcome even the blunders of an obtuse father, our children came through the fire storm just fine. Maybe the experience was even good for them. Who knows.

But their father—he was another story. I was devastated. I was confused. And I was more than a tad angry. Angry that the world was such a cruel, heartless place that it delighted in taking away the innocence of children. But angry, too, with myself, for being such a buffoon. I was an educated man, after all. Why hadn't I seen it coming? What had clouded my vision? What had gone wrong?

A SELF CONSUMED

The answer, of course, was my old ideal concerning self-disclosure. And that started me thinking about the adequacy of my ideal. To what extent is self-disclosure a good thing, anyway? If it's good for me, why wasn't it particularly good for my children? If it was dangerous for them, then why should I hold it up as an ideal for myself? What was the basis for my ideal, after all? Why had I thought it was such a noble objective in the first place? And why had I found it so difficult to achieve?

As I worked through these questions, I concluded that I held my ideal for two basic reasons. One, self-disclosure felt good, at least for awhile. Whenever I managed to get up the courage to reveal a bit of myself to others, it gave me a tremendous sense of relief. Almost a rush. True, it didn't last long. And on some occasions it actually increased my worries. But in the short term, it usually felt pretty good. Secondly, however, it seemed to be good as well. Wasn't self-disclosure simply an attempt at honesty? And isn't honesty a high value for the Christian? How can something that feels and seems so right be anything but right?

It was in pondering that last question, however, that I was required to go beyond simple answers and instant proofs. In part, that was because I had heard that same argument used by my peers to justify their involvement in drugs and sex. If it feels right and seems right, then isn't it? No, I had to admit. Feelings and superficial assumptions can lead one astray. The essential question was not what seemed or felt right, but what indeed was right. So then: What was right in this matter of self-disclosure?

That question led almost immediately to a discovery that I'm sure every ten-year-old is aware of but, for some reason, had just passed me right by: self-disclosure—or the practice of revealing one's innermost thoughts and ideas—is not an absolute good. It is something that is helpful on some occasions and downright mean on others. Indeed, the very same revelation to the same individual can be done for good or evil.

For example, you may be bothered by your spouse's bad breath. An absolute rule concerning self-disclosure, therefore, would suggest that you tell your spouse about it whenever the thought crosses your mind, whether you are singing in the choir, gazing at each other over a romantic meal, or just talking in the privacy of your room. But loving spouses do not do that. Why? Because they understand that there are much higher values than self-disclosure operating in a marriage. And so they engage in a bit of loving repression, holding back their feelings until a time when the revelation will do some good.

Self-disclosure is only honorable under certain circumstances, when it promotes that which is good and right and true. For that reason, outspoken people are appreciated in some situations and not others. We like them when they are willing to look the enemy in the eye and say, "You're wrong." We are not happy when they look us in the eye and say, "You don't sweat much for a fat girl." Self-disclosure requires discernment. It can just as easily be used as a weapon as a bridge. Thus, it is not a value to build one's life upon.

This is so obvious that, when I discovered it, I began wondering why it had taken me so long. Why did I find self-disclosure so attractive, anyway? As I have already said, it felt good and seemed right. But why was I assuming it was an absolute good when, in fact, it was nothing more than a possible means to some other good ends? What accounted for its appeal in the face of such convincing counterevidence?

I had my first clue when I discovered through my studies in sociology that the ideal of self-disclosure is a rather modern notion. It is not something one finds in the great books of the Western world, nor in the traditions of the East for that matter. Neither Peter Peasant nor Larry Lord would have heard of the ideal, and neither of them would have felt particularly good about engaging in it. We Moderns are the ones that think self-disclosure is the cat's pajamas, and we are the ones whose hearts are moved to tears by it.

And that raises the question, Why? Why is self-disclosure such a uniquely modern ideal? The answer, I think, is not so much found in the word "disclosure" but "self." It is self-disclosure that is unusual, not disclosure. Human beings have always been interested in uncovering hidden thoughts and activities, if for no other reason than to get at the truth. No trial could get off the ground without some form of disclosure. What is unusual about us, however, is that we wish to disclose the self. And thus, the real goal of self-disclosure today is not so much to get at the truth but to find the real you. To discover who you "really are" so that you can "be yourself" and live according to the needs of the self.

Now, there are two things that are really quite remarkable about this goal of finding yourself and then attempting to live according to that finding. First, it isn't achievable. It just can't be done. And secondly, from a Christian perspective, is isn't a particularly worthwhile endeavor. Since both of those may seem somewhat controversial, let us look at them in turn.

First, why isn't it possible? Well, the basic problem comes in trying to determine who you really are. Remember, the ideal here is to be yourself. But how can you possibly know what that is? In point of fact, you and I are constantly changing beings. Every day we learn new things, make new friends, and face different situations. These experiences of change make the whole concept of a static self improbable, to say the least. The question immediately becomes, who are you trying to be when you say that you want to be yourself? Who you were yesterday? A year ago? Ten years ago?

And even if you could point to a time in your life that represented your ideal, how could you ever become that person again? You have changed since that time by virtue of the things you have learned and the events you have experienced. Can you undo those experiences? Can you slough off what you have learned? Is it possible for you to become something you assume you once were?

And then there's this matter of playing roles, which we were so repulsed by in the sixties. Often we assumed then, and still assume today, that role playing gets in the way of being ourselves. We say that we are not really the person people see—that we are just playing the roles of mechanic or professor or student—and that beneath those roles is the real us.

But what is the real you? What is the real me? What are you doing on those occasions when you are really you? Is it when you are home in your living room reading the newspaper and scratching your dog behind the ear? That can't be right because then you are playing the role of dog owner and news consumer. Is it when you are hugging your spouse or talking with your children? No, then you are playing the roles of husband or wife and parent. The point is, role playing is very much a part of the warp and woof of life. It is how we get by. How we live. To be human is to learn and participate in a whole variety of roles. Doing so is not being fake, it's being human. Without roles, our lives would be in utter chaos. Indeed, it wouldn't be human life at all.

What all this comes down to is that the search for the true self is a fruitless search, and the desire to transcend roles is a vain desire. Both are destined to lead only to disappointment and failure. And that raises another question: Why do we wish to find ourselves if there is no self to find? And why do we want to leave our roles behind if roles are an essential part of being human?

There are a number of possibilities here, but I will only mention two. First, it is possible that this whole endeavor is really a colossal problem of semantics. In this case, what we mean is not that we are trying to find ourselves, but that we are attempting to become particular kinds of people. Not that we are trying to slip out of roles altogether but simply to find the roles to which we are best suited. Indeed, I've discovered in talking with some people that this is precisely what they mean. And once these folks get their terminology straight, they then appear to be moving along a very realistic path.

The problem is, for most people it is not a semantic problem. And even when it is, the question still remains: Why would we choose to use words that bear little relation to what we actually mean? Why is it that we couch this journey in terms of the self? And why is it that so many people seem to be earnestly on a journey to find it?

The answer, I want to suggest, has nothing at all to do with what is possible but what is believed. And maybe the best way to get at this is to simply begin by saying that this whole business of finding oneself is totally foreign to Holy Scripture. The Bible neither uses that kind of language, nor assumes that kind of worldview, nor instructs us to aspire to that kind of goal. Jesus doesn't ask us to find ourselves; he tells us to follow him. Genesis doesn't start out, "In the beginning, Self" but "In the beginning, God." The dominant figure in Scripture is unmistakably and undeniably God. Everyone else finds their meaning and purpose and direction in him. Or they don't find it.

The desire to find oneself, then, as nice as it may sound, is really not very nice at all. It has the ring of truth because it sounds like someone who is standing up for his own convictions, and we're all impressed with that. Nevertheless, not all convictions are created equal. Some are worth standing up for and some are not. In the end, the question is not whether you are true to your own convictions but whether your convictions are true. If so, standing firm is a worthy objective. If not, you are being loyal to a fault.

So where does this self-preoccupation come from? If it's

neither possible to find nor worthy of pursuit, why do we seek after it? That is a complicated question, worthy of a book, not just a few paragraphs. But the simple answer is that it is rooted in a certain way of thinking and a certain way of living.

The way of thinking can be found throughout human history, but since the eighteenth century it generally assumes the existence of some kind of "natural man," an essential person underneath the layers of moral and social teaching that come with civilization. Stripping away the outer layers, then, allows one to get to the good stuff, after which one can build new layers, more consistent with the good stuff that is naturally there. This idea assumes that human difficulties are not primarily the result of an inner problem but an outer condition, a condition brought about by well-meaning hacks who haven't been enlightened concerning the basic realities of existence.

As in all ideas, there is an element of truth here. Often the training we receive—from parents, preachers, teachers, TV, and society in general—is pretty bad and needs to be undone. But when we are unwrapped (by a therapist, a friend, or whomever), what we discover according to the apostle Paul is not all that wonderful to behold and certainly not the "self" we were looking for. In fact, the natural man—if we can call it that—is a cauldron of good and evil, a reflection of both the image of God and the Fall, and something that is desperately in need of redemption. It is not the solution to our problems but something that must find its solution and purpose in its Creator. The natural man idea may be a convenient way to explain human problems but it is a half truth at best and a dangerous assumption to build one's future upon.

But there is more than philosophy going on here. For we have also developed a way of living that makes it easy for us to put the self at center stage. One of the things that distinguishes us Moderns from our ancestors is that we are a people of choices, determined to control our own lives and use technology to provide us with ever more wonderful options. As we have acquired more choices, however, we have increasingly made self-interest the basis of those choices. Questions such as, "Where should I work, live, go to school?" and "Whom should I live with and befriend?" are not determined by tradition (as in the past) or an attitude of service (as one might hope) but by the modern values of happiness and self-satisfaction. That is, we make such choices in order to find personal fulfillment.

Superficially, that doesn't seem a bad goal. All of us want careers and friends that bring us satisfaction. But with every such decision, we place the self more and more securely on the throne, and we find it more and more reasonable to direct our lives according to its purposes. To seek after the kingdom of self-satisfaction. To believe that when we finally find ourselves, we will be happy.

Does this mean that we should avoid self-disclosure at all times? Is it bad, after all, to reveal ourselves to others? Certainly not. Revealing our deeper thoughts and feelings is a wonderful part of a growing relationship. It is how we get closer to one another. It is how we test out new ideas and learn about the feelings of others toward us. Every kind of therapy—from that which occurs when good friends talk to that which takes place in a psychiatrist's office—requires the ability to unearth aspects of our innermost being.

In the same way, there is nothing wrong with those moments of liberation—such as we had at my advisor's house—when one is suddenly freed up from false expectations. We were trying to be perfect, after all: perfectly charming, perfectly brilliant and perfectly competent in all things human. And of course, we weren't. Judy's trip into the study was clear evidence of that fact. And the liberation I felt when relieved of that false ideal was wonderful. It should have happened long before it did.

The question is, what do you do once you are free of false expectations? And what is the purpose of self-disclosure, anyway? Our world would have us believe that it is to free ourselves from expectations altogether, as if freedom itself was the goal and self-discovery was the key to a joyful existence. Yet it never works out that way. And for good reason. There is no life without expectations and there is no lasting satisfaction in self-disclosure. That is why we break every promise to "just be ourselves" the moment we make it. And that is why the search for self-discovery is never-ending.

In the final analysis, the question is not Who am I? but Whom should I become? And the purpose of freeing ourselves from false expectations is to find better ones. We will not be judged by the depth of our self-understanding, after all, but by the depth of our love for God and neighbor. When self-understanding leads to that goal—as it sometimes can—it is a helpful endeavor. But when self-understanding becomes our end and our overriding purpose in life, it is not a help. It is, in fact, a form of idolatry.

Lord, help me to worry a little less about finding myself. And a little more about finding my direction and resolve in you.

CHAPTER 4
DISCOVERING HOW TO LIVE

THE PAST AS PRESENT

We learned yesterday that Judy's mother has an inoperable form of cancer. She will probably live for only a few more months. Mom has been slowly declining for a year or two now, but we attributed the decline to a stroke she suffered sometime back. So, yesterday's news about the cancer was a complete surprise. And I must confess, I was not ready for it.

I never am. I remember the day that I realized my dad was going to die. At the time, his problems hadn't been fully diagnosed. He had simply felt some numbing in his left leg and had experienced a certain loss of control. The doctor told him that it might be a nerve problem and that he should check into the hospital immediately for tests. Judy and I had just moved to New England, so my folks gave us a call from the old homestead in California, bridging the three-thousand-mile gap in an instant to give us the news.

"Don't worry," Dad said. "I've had back problems for most of my adult life. My guess is the numbness is related to my back condition in some way. We'll give you another call when the test results come in."

He hung up cheerfully, but tears had already begun welling up in my eyes. Though Dad was only in his late fifties and seemed to be in top form, I realized that his symptoms were more serious than he was letting on. And for a reason I can't explain, I just knew

78

that his condition was fatal. I felt it in my bones. Such "knowing" happens to me from time to time. And when it does, I like to think that it is a kind of intuitive knowing, inspired by something beyond a mere hunch. Unfortunately, when I keep track of such "knowings," I discover that they are wrong about half of the time, the logical conclusion being that they are nothing more than educated guesses stirred up by a little adrenaline. Consequently, I no longer keep track.

Anyway, this time there was no reason to keep track. I had no doubt about the future. As I hung up the phone and slumped down on the couch in the living room, I knew that I was going to lose my father. Everything from the knot in my stomach to the gray January sky seemed to confirm it. The man who was so strong that he would have confronted the king of England if truth were at stake, but so weak that he turned green at the sight of dead cats even though he didn't like cats—that man, my father, was going to leave me. And I was not ready for him to go.

And now it was Judy's mom's turn. Those same feelings of unpreparedness were bubbling up to the surface once again. It was not pity. Both my dad and Judy's mom have been blessed of God. I cannot say, as many have, that "it's not fair." Not when the God who now permits their death, also lavished on them the Good News of Jesus Christ, drawing them to himself, and using them to serve others in his name, feeding the hungry, mending the brokenhearted, and leading the dying to a knowledge of new life. True, I wish they wouldn't have to suffer the agony and pain of death. But that is the lot of us all, we of Adam's race. And for inheritors of the Fall, Mom and Dad have done pretty well.

No, it is not their condition or destiny that bothers me so. It is "me" that bothers me so. What I am going to have to give up. And what I have failed to fully appreciate along the way.

The problem was brought home to me while listening to an old Simon and Garfunkel tune last night. That may seem odd and even somewhat sacrilegious given this discussion, especially since neither Mom nor Dad would have much appreciated this duo. Had you mentioned the name of Simon and Garfunkel to them, I'm sure they would have thought you were talking about a piano company. Or possibly a high quality cleaning agent. They were not much into the sixties as a cultural event—being rather hard at work trying to nourish and cope with children who were—and assumed that the "Sounds of Silence" was a welcome relief from the stuff that bellowed out of their offspring's bedrooms.

Nevertheless, Mom, Dad, and Simon and Garfunkel all came together for me last night when our local PBS station decided to run a concert instead of the late-night news. This is pledge week, it turns out, and whenever they need donations at PBS in Boston, you start seeing a lot of James Taylor, *Brideshead Revisited,* and *The World at War* (sort of a mellow, literate, historical approach to rock, sex, and violence). And of course, Simon and Garfunkel. Before I had a chance to switch the channel, then, "parsley, sage, rosemary, and thyme" began wafting its way into the room. And within moments, I was absolutely immobilized. Transfixed. Not by the music, but by the memories. For suddenly, there I was—back in college—dating Judy and twenty years old all over again. And, too, there was Mom. And Dad.

I was simply there, twenty years earlier in my life—seeing people, capturing smiles and laughter, images and smells—using all of my senses, in other words, to take in the moment. Now, don't misunderstand me here. This was not some kind of New Age, Shirley MacLainian, neo-Hindu, mystical experience. I was not a disembodied spirit, moving around in space and time. I never left the room. Nevertheless, the past was suddenly present for me. And the feelings and sensations of a bygone era were incredibly real.

Such an experience cannot be fully captured in words, if only because the images and feelings are so disconnected. Again, it wasn't a story. Rather, it was the image of the sun, going down over the harbor in Santa Barbara while Judy and I were curving our way along Milpas Road. That would be followed by the smells and tastes of ice cream, or the image of Judy with a smidgen of vanilla on the tip of her Brinkman nose, laughing so hard that she couldn't lift her hand to wipe it off, nor hide her beautiful smile, inside of which are teeth so white they make the ice cream look yellow. And my heart melt.

And then, all of the sudden, there was Judy's mom. Forty-five and going on nineteen, with a teeny-bopper's figure and a giggle to match. Standing in the kitchen, I could hear the garage door open as Judy's dad came home from work. Sweet Old Bill, as the family had named him—precisely because the acronym was so wrong and the words so right—was soon bouncing out of the car and into the front door, forever with a huge smile on his face and something sweet in his hand, eager to hug the woman that God had given him. And the woman? Always at the door. Always surprised by the chocolates. Always ambushed by the kiss. Always embarrassed by the attention. And always absolutely loving the whole bloomin' ritual.

Ah, but this won't do. You can't see her. You can't see the way she held her body in reserve while she let her eyes do the talking, feigning shyness with her manner but going right for the jugular with her look. Those eyes. Those eyes! As beautiful as any I have seen in my life. Bluer than a Kansas sky in May, they could dance and sing and laugh in a way that the rest of her just could not. Nor needed to. Because everything you needed to know was right there in her eyes. Unguarded. Unpretentious. And unable to communicate anything but what she believed in the depths of her soul.

Still, I struggle with words. Maybe an incident will help. I remember the day Judy and I told her mom and dad about our engagement—no, "asked for the right to marry," would be the more accurate way of saying it. Actually, we were a bit confused about the whole procedure, having been bounced around by the teachings of traditionalists as well as counter-culture types. The old standard approach, whereby the fiancé asks the father for his daughter's hand in marriage, didn't seem quite right. I could never

CHAPTER 4

understand why the men in the household had the prerogative to
go off someplace and seal the marital fate of women. On the other
hand, the modern notion of couples simply announcing their
wedding plans to their parents seemed equally unjust, not to
mention disrespectful. After all, we were still under the care of our
parents. Didn't they deserve some say in the matter?

Well, we resolved the dilemma by bringing both Judy's
mom and dad into the kitchen at the same time, and asking
them—together—for the right to get married. That sounds all
rather matter-of-fact, as if we simply danced in and asked the
question. In point of fact, I was quivering in my penny loafers.
The problem, you see, is that Judy and I had been dating for only
about five months. On the surface, then, it looked as if we had
simply met, gone googlie-eyed over each other, and decided
impulsively and immediately thereafter to get married. And that's
pretty much how it looked below the surface, as well. Except that
we had both had previous experiences that had prepared us for one
another. And we knew (in our bones, again) that this was right.

But that didn't mean anyone else would think it was right.
Especially not parents, who are charged with the responsibility of
looking after the long-term needs and interests of their children.
So when we finally faced them in the kitchen, I was a bit worried.
And with good reason. They had every right to say, "Slow down.
You're moving too fast. Give this thing a little more time to cook
and for you to get to know one another a little better. Why don't
you both finish college first, at least, and then see if the marital
urge is still with you?" That's what they had a right to say,
anyway. It is most likely the kind of thing that I would have said if
I were in their shoes.

But that is not what they said, probably because they were a
lot smarter than I am. Instead, when we popped the question, they
both broke out into huge grins, grabbed each other's hands, and
said . . . actually, I don't even remember what they said! What I
recall, however, is what they did. How their grins filled their
faces. How Mom's eyes absolutely sparkled with wonder and

satisfaction. How Mom and Dad kept looking back and forth, from us to one another, communicating in their manner—not only their happiness for us—but also their joy and delight in their own marriage. "How could we say no?" was the question that radiated from their faces. As if marriage had been so good for them they couldn't think of depriving anyone else of that same joy.

What a gift their faces were to us on that day. Not only because they offered us a badly needed blessing, but because they mirrored to us the joyful possibilities of marriage itself. It wasn't the "yes, but be careful" response we deserved, after which there should have come a hundred warnings about the dangers of marriage in the modern world. It was, rather, a "yes, and be grateful" response. Be grateful that God has given you to one another. Be grateful for the institution of marriage itself. Be grateful, as we are, for the gift of love between a man and woman. And most of all? Enjoy. Enjoy this gift that God has given you.

And so we did. In no small measure because of the model of love and affection that Mom and Dad lived out in front of us in their own marriage. A model that still stands out as bright and clear as the day I first encountered it. Especially when I hear Simon and Garfunkel.

The song ends and another takes its place. And without the least concern for logic or story line, my own father appears. Not as he was in the last few months of his life, when the stroke left him partially immobilized and confined to a wheelchair. But how he was for the thirty years I knew him. Quick. Lean. And tall. Always tall. Always taller than me! Why was that anyway? Just a genetic quirk? Or could it be a metaphor of our relationship?

All my life, people told me about my father's height. They did this in order to encourage me, I think. The line was that my dad had been a short, skinny kid, just like myself. But then, suddenly, when he was a senior in high school, he shot up like a rocket. He became tall in a matter of minutes, I surmised. And so I waited to get tall as well. Especially during my senior year in high school, I must have looked at myself in the mirror three times a day, just to see whether I was tall yet. But alas, I remained average. Barely six feet when I stretched. And still terribly skinny. I never would match my dad in stature.

And I don't ever remember minding. Which is a surprise, now that I think of it. Because I certainly wanted to be tall. Every time I went in for a lay-up, or tried an overhead smash, or looked at Cheryl Tieggs, I wanted to be tall. But I never minded being shorter than Dad. That was always the concern of others, not mine. For me, there was always something comforting and right about his stature. I was simply no match for him and, to be honest with you, I kind of liked it that way.

Delivering potatoes, now. Me, thirteen years old and sitting in the driver's seat of Dad's pickup, barely able to look over the steering wheel but driving right through the middle of town, nevertheless. Why this abuse of California traffic regulations? Because Dad is sitting in the back of the pickup, delivering 100-pound bags of potatoes to an assortment of friends, relatives, and needy citizens. Even for a legalist, some things are more important than law. And so, three years before I was qualified for a license, I was meandering around the streets of town in my dad's pickup, while he ran back and forth—from pickup to house and back again—toting those hundred pound bags on his shoulders, and delivering the fruit of his labor to those he loved.

And again, I didn't mind being smaller than Dad. The bags were heavy, for one thing. And it was only my size that protected me from lugging those gunnysacks and put me in the driver's seat instead. But there was something else, as well. I simply wasn't up to the task of knocking on people's doors and giving them a sack of potatoes. It seemed embarrassing to me. Below my dignity, not to mention my dad's. Here was my father, after all, a fairly successful farmer, with land and employees and social standing, running around town with sacks of potatoes on his shoulder, making a spectacle of himself. Why didn't he pay someone else to deliver them? Why did he have to take the time and energy to cart these crazy potatoes around town himself?

I was smaller than Dad and yet it was beneath my dignity to be generous to others. Dad, on the other hand, was tall. And yet, he had no difficulty whatsoever putting others above himself. It was easy for him to be small, in other words. And I think that's why God made him tall. Very, very tall.

And as Simon and Garfunkel kept at it, in my mind's eye, my dad kept at it as well. Delivering potatoes. Entrusting me with responsibilities (like driving a pickup) long before I deserved to be so trusted. Letting me tag along with him, even though he knew I would get in the way. Just being tall. Very, very tall.

THE PRESENT AS FUTURE

Two things strike me as I think about these images that Simon and Garfunkel evoked last night. First, there seems to be a vast difference between what I was thinking at the time these images were created and what I am thinking now. And second, those images just don't seem to go away.

About the first, I have often been struck before. Why is it that when I interact with other people, I am almost completely consumed with myself—what I am trying to accomplish, where I am going, how I appear to them—that sort of thing? But later on, when I reflect upon these same moments of interaction, I have a hard time even remembering what I was wearing or doing? What I remember, instead, are those other people—what they were wearing, how they looked, and how they responded to me. Why is it that in the present I am consumed by my objectives, while my memories are made up almost entirely of people?

Take the potato delivery episode with my dad, for example. The first thing that came to mind was my father, lugging those sacks on his shoulders, smiling his nervous grin and being very tall. That was absolutely clear. My own role in the situation I can remember only in relation to him: that I was driving for him and feeling a bit embarrassed by the whole thing. What I cannot even bring to mind are those things that were consuming my life at the time, whether it might have been hitting a home run at the next baseball game or striking out with my girlfriend (assuming I had one). What I do know—because it is still true today—is that I was not making the most of the moment, nor was I thinking much about the man who was delivering the potatoes. I had other, more important things to think about. Like whether or not I could hit Mark Larson's fastball.

And it's all quite ludicrous, isn't it? Just as silly as the fact that this afternoon I will be talking with students in my office and thinking about how I am going to be able to finish this chapter by the end of the week. Or talking with my children at the dinner table tonight and thinking about how I am going to finish my Brussels sprouts. The problem, of course, isn't thinking about my duties as an author or a consumer. Those tasks require thought and deliberation. They have their place. The question is, why do I let those objectives crowd in on my time with people? In a few months, if not weeks, I won't even remember what those objectives were. And yet, today, I have a hard time setting them aside for people—for the only thing that will matter much to me as time goes by. Why is that?

As a behavioral scientist, I can think of lots of answers, all of which would probably be helpful but all of which would no doubt miss the mark as well. Because the answer is not so much a matter of how we remember or perceive or recall, but how we live our lives. And if I am representative of the human race, we pretty much spend our time pursuing those tangible items we assume will bring us the most satisfaction. Professors think about books in the middle of a conversation with a student because everybody reads books and only God reads a conversation. Fathers give more attention to their Brussels sprouts than their children because stomachs are sometimes more demanding than loved ones.

And children? Well, this child, anyway, was a lot more concerned with the admiration of his peers on the baseball field than he was in appreciating the man who deserved his admiration. I say that, by the way, not out of a false sense of guilt (very few thirteen-year-olds are able to transcend adolescent self indulgence). Rather, I say it with regret. With sorrow. Because I was the loser in the whole thing, not my dad. He had plenty to do just trying to get those potato sacks to the right door. He didn't need my appreciation. But I needed it. I was the one who was so preoccupied with myself that I couldn't take the time to enjoy the one who was worthy of my enjoyment. And, by making that choice, I really didn't serve myself well in the end. I robbed myself of the joy I was seeking.

But not completely. Because my heart is a lot smarter than I am. And rather than remembering the trivia that occupies my daily life, my heart stores up real treasure instead—memories of people, as well as sights and sounds and smells, that will be of value to me throughout eternity. I am thankful for my heart. Its affections and insights are a genuine gift of God. But, oh, how I wish I could get my life more in sync with my heart! Maybe then I might actually appreciate the treasures God gives me on the day they are delivered—rather than twenty years down the road.

The second thing that strikes me about those memories is that they just don't seem to go away. Though the people and places might have disappeared, the memories are as vivid as the day they were made. In fact, let me state it more strongly: Though the people are gone, they are not gone. Though the sounds and smells and sights have vanished from the face of the earth, they continue to exist. You may say, "Oh sure, they exist in your mind; but they don't *really* exist anymore." But that won't do. Because they were significant to me in the first place only because they existed in my mind. Had my mind not encountered them, they wouldn't have had any effect on me.

For example, the Sierra Nevada mountains exist. God created them and they exist in all their majesty and beauty and splendor regardless of whether or not I ever encounter them. But the only way they become significant for me is if I experience them personally. Once I have hiked through them, smelled the pine trees early in the morning, or crimped my neck trying to see the mountain peaks, then they become a part of my being. They become a part of my existence.

The interesting thing, however, is that they continue to be a part of my existence whether or not I stay in the mountains. That is, I continue to experience them as real, even though I now live thousands of miles away on the shores of a distant ocean. Those mountains are every bit as real for me today as they were the first time I encountered them. And that is not just something I say to make myself feel good or to engage in a bit of nostalgic reverie. It is, in fact, precisely true. I experience them today just as I did in the first place.

The point is, my memories of Judy's mom and my father are not "mere memories," as we tend to think of the term. They are not simply dreamy states of mind that bear little relation to the actual event. They *are* the actual event, recurring again and again, with every bit as much reality and force as they originally had. Mom and Dad exist today, just as they did twenty years ago, when Mom was standing by the door waiting for the happy homecoming of her husband, and Dad was towering over me in all his generosity, humility, and height. Mom and Dad still remain.

That was captured well, I think, by my Uncle Harold on the day of my father's funeral. It had been a beautiful, sunny December day. As is the custom in my home church, the funeral service was immediately followed by a graveside service, at which time the body is committed to the ground and the person is finally given back to his Creator. It is a good time for the family because it is a visual reminder that the body has returned to the earth. But it is a hard time, as well, because what you are seeing with your eyes is hard to comprehend with your heart.

And Uncle Harold must have been thinking precisely that. Because as we lingered around the graveside for a final few minutes, he looked at me, his face oozing with a mixture of incredulity and pain, and said, "I just can't believe he's gone." It was a poignant moment for me. Because here was a man who had known my dad since the day the two of them were grafted into the Unruh clan through marriage, as much peas in a pod as any two unrelated relatives could be. They were both children of the Depression. Both, indeed, had gone through hard times, started their own businesses and, as a result, now earned their livelihood by worrying and expending huge amounts of energy. But they were also pretty smart. Smart enough, in fact, to marry into the Unruh clan, a people who—though capable of fair amounts of worry themselves—were more prone to laughter and optimism and enjoyment.

Most importantly, Harold and my dad were individualists while the Unruh clan consisted of a bunch of groupies, people who loved nothing more than being together, swapping stories and eating Grandma's chicken dinners. It was a wild combination—these individualists in the midst of the groupie Unruhs—but on the whole, it was a great blessing. Certainly, it was a blessing for Harold and my dad, since it forced them to be with others when their natural tendency would have been to go off by themselves and work a bit more. But it was also a blessing to me, because it meant that I was nurtured in an environment that included both achievement and security, individual ambition as well as a strong sense of belonging and attachment.

But at this moment, standing there at the graveside of my father, it meant that Uncle Harold had lost the other individualist in the family. In the midst of his loss, I think he understood that he was not an individualist after all—that he too needed others. Such a loss is hard to take. In fact, the death of those we love is hard to believe. And so, looking at that casket, which contained the body of his friend and my father, he uttered those most comprehensible of incomprehensibilities, "I can't believe he's gone."

And yet—as I say this, the chills run down my spine—and yet, in just a few short years, Uncle Harold was gone too, taken by a heart attack long before his time. The man who couldn't

THE PRESENT AS FUTURE

believe my father was gone, is also gone. And the whole thing seems absolutely ridiculous to me. Absurd. How can my father be gone in the first place? And how can the one who was, only moments before, disbelieving my father's passing, also have passed from the scene? Of course, I understand the history of the thing. Two men died, one right after the other. That's easy to understand. What is not fathomable to me, however, is that they no longer exist. That they are gone. They are as much a part of me now as they were twenty years ago. How can they, then, be gone?

That question, along with its obvious answer—that they are not gone, that their being persists in spite of the death of their bodies—is the bane of naturalists everywhere. A naturalistic worldview, of course, asserts that the material world is the sum total of reality. For the naturalist, then, the physical death of anything is the end because there isn't anything else. This way of thinking makes a great deal of sense in a consumptive society such as our own, where we are prone to use things up quickly, get rid of them, and then buy something new to take their place. In such a society, destruction is normal and even a bit comforting. It is nice to believe that your garbage is behind you.

But even in a materialistic society, a naturalistic worldview is really very difficult to sustain. The things we destroy keep coming back to haunt us, for one thing, be they disposable diapers or carbon monoxide or radioactive waste. Life seems to remind us, even against our will, that things are not easily discarded. Things seem to persist in one form or another, regardless of how hard we try to destroy them. Out of sight is not out of mind. But just as importantly, there are some things that we don't want to lose. Like that giant elm tree in the front yard. Or that favorite pet around the house. Or to bring it all close to home, like friends and family members who are dear to the heart. Those are things we would do anything to keep. And those are things we just can't bring ourselves to believe are really gone.

The naturalist, of course, says, "Tough beans! Facts are not built on wishes. And the fact of the matter is, those things are gone." But the heart is not satisfied with such a materialistic definition of "fact." Its facts include the experiences of climbing that giant elm tree, of burying your head in the paws of your cocker spaniel, of hugging and crying and laughing with the one you love. And those experiences persist, even when the tree, the pet, or the loved one is no longer within reach. The thing which caused the heart to sing in the first place may be absent, but the heart goes on singing just the same. And its song is as real today as the moment it was learned.

The problem with naturalism, then, is that it just isn't believable. Things linger beyond their physical existence. Dad isn't, and yet he is. There's the problem. Naturalism has an answer, of course: that Dad is only an image in my brain, a mere mental construct. But that hardly seems satisfactory. Why is it that my brain can retain images past their time—enabling me to talk about them, hold on to them, cherish them? Of course, naturalism can supply another material answer, for which another "why" question will pop up. But in this regress of question and answer, naturalism will lose. Must lose. Because the number of material answers available is finite, while the why question is infinite. For every natural answer, the heart that God gave us will want to know why. And will, eventually, seek its answers in more fertile soil.

That was illustrated nicely, I think, in the movie *Somewhere in Time*. For those of you who missed this box office flop, it's about a young man who falls in love with a woman who lived during a previous era. That may seem like quite a trick but, in Hollywood, all things are possible. And in this case, the young man manages to go back in time, find the woman of his dreams, convince her that his love is true, and win her heart in the process. It is all very romantic and sappy and all that good stuff until, suddenly, against his will, he is instantly transported back to his own time period. As a result, he finds himself stuck in his own era, tragically separated from the love of his life. She is lost Somewhere in Time. And he is lost without her love.

THE PRESENT AS FUTURE

What we have here is the classic, tragic love story but with a twist. Instead of family or war or religion coming between the star-struck couple, it is time. They are people of two different eras, denied the pleasure of one another's company by the simple existence of time. It is a tragedy, to be sure. But the interesting thing to me is that their predicament is not merely the tragedy of this sappy love story. It is, in fact, the tragedy of us all. Because each of us, regardless of our age or era, are the victims of time where love is concerned.

This is true for a very simple reason: Every moment of love is lost in time. This is the case even when the one we loved yesterday is still with us today. From the perspective of time, it is not possible to retrieve the moment of affection we had yesterday, whether it involved hugging our grandmother, our child, or our spouse. We can, of course, hug them again today, and that experience may be better or worse. But it will be different. And it will not bring back what occurred the day before.

None of this is particularly troubling, of course, until the one we love leaves us permanently, as is the case in death. For then, suddenly, we are no longer in the position of even being able to create new moments of love. We are simply left with past events that can never be recreated. But time marches on, the heartless master of our every act of love, methodically taking them away from us, like an ocean wave pulling a life raft ever farther away from your fingertips. And we? What can we do? Absolutely nothing. Except watch the event fade into the distance. And cry.

But our hearts will not allow us to leave it at that. Love remembers the person, in all their fullness and humanity, and finds the nonexistence of that person to be unthinkable. In fact, to love, it doesn't make sense. From the perspective of time, however, it makes perfect sense. From the perspective of time, it is love that doesn't make sense. Love—as anything more than a momentary feeling—is really just a convenient fiction. Something happens and then it's gone. Time stands with us as we look at the coffins of our loved ones and says, "He's gone. It's over. What's next?"

CHAPTER 4

Love, on the other hand, utters the words of my Uncle Harold, "I can't believe he's gone." It is not believable to love because love goes right on loving regardless of what happens in time. From the perspective of love, my dad is still there in all his humanness, enabling me to love him and feel his love in return. That means, then, that for love, time is a fiction. It pretends to separate us from something that never leaves us, to kill something that never dies. And so it can't be true.

The question, of course, is which perspective is correct? Is it time's? Or love's? They cannot both be true and yet they both exert an influence on our lives that is undeniable, a presence too real to deny. Those who deny time must imagine away that dead remains in front of them—in all its stinking, rotting reality. That is a feat too fraudulent for most mortals to go along with. Those who dismiss love, on the other hand, must now learn to live without it; to befriend, to serve a neighbor, to hug a child or consummate a marriage, and admit that it's all quite meaningless. That is an admission too absurd for most mortals to bear. Eternal life, you see, is not some illogical concoction we have come up with because we want to live forever. Quite the reverse. We believe in eternity because it is the only logical way of making sense out of our lives now.

And so we live with them both, don't we, these contradictions in meaning and purpose. Not being able to deny what either our hearts or eyes are telling us, we live with the tension of believing them both. But we also live with the knowledge that one day the tension will be resolved. For not only do we have to live with the deaths of those around us, but we must also contemplate our own. And on that day, either time will win and love will be meaningless, or love will win and time will be no more.

Another call from California. And now I hear the words I can't believe, "She's gone." Shirley Mae B. Wright, Judy's mother, is dead.

But how can that be, anyway? Let me say it again, in the

strongest possible terms: *How can that be?* I can see her there, sitting at the table in front of us. Her eyes, full of mischief and delight, saying to Judy and me, "Of course you two can get married. God has given you to one another, hasn't he? He has put his love deep within you and offered you the opportunity to love one another as result. Why wouldn't we allow you to get married? Why, in heaven's name, would we want to deny you such a love?"

Why, indeed? Why would anyone deny such a love? And how?

Mom is gone and I can't believe it. And for the love of God, *I do not!*

THE FUTURE AS NOW

And then what? My conclusion—that love is the larger reality that will someday put time in its place—is not a novel one. It is the conclusion that most people draw, especially during times of grief or great joy. Without it, there is no solace at a funeral nor much meaning in a wedding vow. And so, when the time is right, we are all inclined to give love its due.

But what about the rest of the time? Or more generally, once we give love preeminence, what do we do with it? Where do we go from there?

That was the question that came to mind while listening to the chaplain at West Point Military Academy the other day. Actually, when he began his talk, my mind wasn't consumed with anything so grand as questions of love or eternity. I was rather in a deep funk about the override our town is trying to get passed in order to compensate for a state budget problem. I won't bore you with details, but a downturn in the economy has left our state government in deficit. To deal with that problem, the state has reduced its allocations to cities and towns. That means that we need to increase our local property taxes to compensate for the shortfall from the state. And that requires voter approval. Without it, our schools will have to drastically cut programs and people.

Now, you should know that I am in favor of the tax

override. I would far rather pay a few more dollars in property taxes than see foreign languages get cut or the co-curricular program gutted. But to be honest, I see the validity of the opponents' position as well. Some people just can't afford an increase in their property taxes right now, especially the elderly who are living on fixed incomes. They bought their homes many years ago, when housing costs were low and when they were earning a healthy income. Since then, however, housing costs have skyrocketed—along with property taxes—but their incomes have remained stranded on the launching pad. As a result, many of them can hardly afford to stay in their homes. And that's not fair.

What this means, in other words, is that this decision (like all decisions in the political arena) will help some people and hurt others, regardless of the outcome. And that I understand. What has me feeling blue, however, are the arguments people use to support their positions, and the motivations and values revealed therein. For in the heat of debate, people not only say some things they don't mean, they also sometimes say exactly what they mean, a meaning often hidden in everyday life by the guise of civility and tolerance. And the revelations in this debate are heartbreaking.

Just yesterday, a man who was against the tax increase was interviewed on the local television station. He was asked, "Are you going to vote for the override?" His answer was quick and unabridged. "Of course not," he said. "I haven't had kids in school for over twenty years now. Why should I vote to have my taxes increased?" His words were direct but his demeanor was even more aggressive. From his expression, you would have thought he had been asked about the validity of shooting his mother. He was absolutely incredulous.

And so was I in response. "What is happening to our world, Judy?" I asked in my typical understated way. "How can people be so incredibly self-centered?" I jumped up from the floor to turn off the television set but kept my mouth in the "On" position. "How can they make a decision that will effect all the children of this community purely on the basis of whether or not it will benefit them personally?"

Now, I have to admit that I have a tendency to extrapolate from the problems of one man to the problems of the whole world. It makes them seem more important. But in this case I wasn't exaggerating. It seemed to me that people are increasingly willing to make public policy decisions on the basis of their own self-interest. If it's good for me, I'll vote for it. If it isn't, I won't. It's as simple as that. Political scientists have long noted the tendency of groups of people to vote in their own self-interest. That is nothing new. But in the past, people at least tried to cover it up with grand, moral arguments. Today, no one even seems to care about the ethics of an issue, or understand that they exist. The only question is, What's in it for me? And that's the whole of the matter.

I was reminded of a society I had studied in anthropology, where the people made many of their decisions on the basis of "amoral familism." For these people, the only important thing in life was the family. In fact, the family was so valuable, that it became the gauge by which every issue was evaluated. For example, if the town wanted to build a park, the only important question was, "Will our family directly benefit?" If so, they were for it; if not, they would oppose it. This same approach was taken to all community projects, from sewage disposal, to water works, to whatever. And do you know what happened? Almost nothing. Because on every single issue, a majority of families concluded that, for them, the costs outweighed the benefits. And as a result, they lived with sewage in the street and without parks or running water, the victims of a worldview that had turned their families into gods and their community into shambles.

As I listened to that man on the news, I wondered if our fate might not be the same. Have we become a people so consumed with our own self-interest that we are no longer able to care about the common good? Do we dare ask anymore, "What is right? Or fair? Or good?" Do we even care—can we even imagine—what

God might think of the matter? Or have those become meaningless questions to us, sacrificed on the altar of selfish ambition and
personal success? Of course, as is always the case in such
circumstances, I had worked myself into a dither over the matter,
and that spilled over into other areas of my life.

"Dad, can I have the car this afternoon after school?" my
daughter innocently asked.

I whirled, a fencer prepared for combat: "Why do you need
the car all the time? All you ever think about is yourself. There are
five people in this family, of which you are only one. We have
only two vehicles, of which only one works consistently. Count it
up! Five people. Two or less cars. Doesn't add up, does it?"

"Uh, Dad," Heather responded gently, "there are only three
drivers. And both cars are working fine, right now. Besides, aren't
you and Mom going to an ordination service this afternoon? You
won't both need a car for that, will you?"

"How do you know what our needs are? Are you ever here?
Do you know how hard we have to work, just to keep this family
above sea level? Do you know what it's like grading a hundred
exams in an evening? Do you know what your mom goes through
all day long? Do you have any idea . . . ?"

"Uh, Dad? Look. You're wonderful. I appreciate all you do
for the family. Blessed am I among daughters. I'll never get home
after 9:00 P.M. again. Etc., etc. Now, can I have the car?"

"Just like that, is it? A few kind words and everything is
hunky-dory. Do you think that's what I want? A little praise?
That's what's wrong with kids these days. They think a few words
can make up for a life of self-indulgent living. Why, when I was
your age, I—"

"Excuse me, Dad, excuse me! When you were my age you
had your own car, you drove yourself to school every day, you
had no curfew, and you pretty much did whatever you wanted.
That's what Grandma says!"

"Well . . . Grandma may be exaggerating a bit. Besides, I
grew up on a farm. You had to have a car on the farm to survive.

CHAPTER 4

And kids were a lot more responsible in those days. Why, we used to—"

"—what you used to do, Grandma says, is drive through the grape orchards and shoot rabbits from the back of a pickup truck with a twelve-gauge shotgun. Sounds pretty responsible to me, Dad. I'm sure the rabbits had it coming too. Everything deserves to die with 5,000 shotgun pellets in its body. Grandma also says—"

"Grandma is not a part of this argument! And I'm not either! Uh . . . well . . . I am part of this argument. But I shouldn't be! I mean, I shouldn't have to defend myself like this. The issue is—"

"The issue is we have to go to the ordination service right now," Judy interrupted as she came floating down the stairs. "Heather, you're going to need the car this afternoon so you can pick up Kirsten from the YMCA. We'll eat at 6:00. Okay?"

"Sure, Mom," Heather responded, as she glided past me. She looked like a gladiator who had just bested ten lions in the arena and was basking in the applause of the crowd. I felt like one of the lions.

And I was still feeling like a lion, sitting there at the ordination service, listening to the chaplain from West Point talk about living the Christian life. But it wasn't the verbal abuse from my family that was getting me down. I had that coming, after all. Anyone who projects the problems of the world onto his children deserves all the verbal abuse he can get. The problem was not that I lost the debate. The problem was that I couldn't get that taxpayer's words out of my head: "I haven't had kids in school for over twenty years now. Why should I vote to have my taxes increased?" How could someone say such a thing? I thought to myself again and again.

Somewhere in the midst of my gloom, the chaplain began to tell a story. Funny thing about stories. They always seem to break into your chain of thought. I can be politely listening to a speaker for an hour or so, nodding my head appropriately and not hearing a word that is being said. But the minute the speaker tells a story—regardless of how deeply I may be immersed in my own thoughts—my mind snaps to attention and I listen. Of course, I don't have any idea how the story fits into the speech. But I listen.

The story (apparently true) was about two West Point cadets of very different abilities and talents. One was athletic and a top-notch scholar—precisely the kind of person everyone wants at the Academy—and the other was a fairly normal fellow without much in the way of athletic ability. This meant that the second fellow had a problem that the first cadet did not. Because to graduate from West Point, seniors must be able to pass a physical fitness test, which includes a certain number of push-ups, sit-ups, and a two-mile run, the latter having to be accomplished in a set amount of time.

As it turns out, these two cadets happened to be taking the test on the same day. For the first cadet, the test was absolutely no problem. For the second, however, it was not only a problem, it was the problem of his life. For if he failed the test, he would not be graduating from West Point in May, if ever. Well, he did manage to pass the first two test items. The two-mile run was a different story, however. He had never run the event within the allotted time and he had no reason to believe that he could do it now. As he proceeded with the run, therefore, he was not full of confidence or hope. And it showed. The further along he went, the more hopeless the thing became, and the more he felt sapped of energy and strength.

Just about the time he was ready to give up, the first cadet—who was running in the same heat—noticed the predicament of the second, and decided to give him some help. This was not an easy decision, by the way, because it meant that he would lose valuable time, and that, in turn, would cost him points in his overall standing in his class. But apparently he concluded that it was worth it. And so, instead of going for a record on the two-mile run, the first cadet slowed down, waited for the second cadet to catch up to him, and then proceeded to encourage him down the track with shouts of, "You can do it." "Go for it." "You're gonna make it." And so on.

Well, the second cadet did not respond with any great burst of speed but he didn't give up either. With the first cadet matching him stride for stride, he continued to plod along, pushing himself for all he was worth. And so it went. The first cadet kept yelling. And he kept running. And with all the energy he could muster, he finally crossed the finish line, the first cadet still at his side, and the second cadet totally spent and exhausted. It would have been a grand moment in history, a made for television spectacle, if not for one thing: neither cadet accomplished the run in the allotted time. They both failed the test.

Not a good story for television is it? Wrong ending. Bad conclusion. But as I listened to the chaplain tell it, I concluded that it was a wonderful story, nevertheless. An awful, wonderful story. Awful, because these two young men did not reap the reward their effort and good intentions deserved. It doesn't seem fair. It flies in the face of our need for cosmic justice. Nevertheless, I think it is a wonderful story too, because it is as clear an illustration of the implications of eternity as one could find.

You see, the first cadet believed in the reality of love over time. And he believed it not simply when it was convenient—not just when he needed a little comfort to get him through his grief, or a little meaning to make his life seem worthwhile. He believed it when it was costly as well. Indeed, he believed it at precisely that moment when time was of the essence, when the stopwatch was running, and when the world said you've got to meet the deadline. At that moment, he said no to time and yes to love.

Thinking about the story, it dawned on me that the cadet didn't deny the importance of time, or its reality. Only its ultimate significance. That is clear from the fact that he was trying to help another human being in his own struggle with time. The goal of the event, after all, was to beat the clock. But what he did was give up that goal for himself in order to help someone else achieve it.

And in that act, he denied the ultimate reality of the thing he was trying to achieve. And put love back on the throne.

Our inclination, of course, is to mourn the outcome of the story. But that merely shows how utterly cockeyed our thinking has become. For what would have been achieved if they had won the race? Merely one more moment of victory, quickly eclipsed by the march of time and followed almost immediately by the demand to meet additional objectives. More realistically, what would have happened if the first cadet had not sacrificed his victory for the second, if he had gone on to succeed while the second had succumbed to lonely defeat? The utter triumph of time, grinding the face of the defeated in its own reality while denying the winner any kind of long-term satisfaction.

But our hero would have none of that. By losing for love's sake, he managed to gain the only victory worth having. And instead of leaving the loser in the dust, to wallow in ignominious defeat, he gave him something worth living for. "He is no fool who loses what he cannot keep to gain that which cannot be lost," in the words of Jim Elliot.

I left the ordination service, no longer thinking of the taxpayer but thinking of myself instead. And that's where my thoughts remain. Today, Judy's mom dies and I declare grandly, love is eternal. And I believe it. But what will happen tomorrow? Time will sound the alarm clock and I will struggle out of bed in obedience, regardless of whether or not my wife needs a hug. I will then go through the day, using all kinds of deadlines as an excuse to ignore the needs of others—grousing appropriately about "the demands on my time" but conveniently forgetting that the demands are self-imposed and designed primarily for my own success.

"But Stan, you have responsibilities," my brain reminds me. Of course, I do. It is no good meeting the need of my wife for a morning hug if it means that we forget about the needs of our children to get to school on time, or I miss my first-period lecture (assuming we get carried away with the hug!). To a certain extent, love is hemmed in by time. I cannot love my wife adequately—as well as children, neighbors, students, brothers, and sisters—if I do not manage my time well. Love, in this life anyway, must be expressed in time.

But so many of my decisions are not like this. They are not a matter of responsibility but self-interest. Like the West Point cadets, I am trying to win the race against time. So I can earn points, graduate, and find my place in the world. In such circumstances, the compelling motive is not service, for I am simply serving myself. And the paramount reality is anything but love.

I am reminded again of the taxpayer who said he wouldn't vote for new taxes since he didn't have any children in school. By implication, of course, he was saying that he would vote differently if he could benefit from it. In other words, he believes in love when it is convenient. The question is, am I really much different? I believe in love when a loved one dies, when I need the comfort. But what about those times when acting in love isn't comfortable? What about those times when love will cost me the race? Do I love like the cadet? Or the taxpayer?

I'll tell you what, the answer had better be, "Like the cadet." Not just because my moral training demands it, but because nothing less than the reality of eternity hangs in the balance. You see, either I live out on the race track of life what I believe at the funeral service, or the funeral service is a sham and a fraud. It's as simple as that. And just as important.

CHAPTER 5
DISCOVERING WHAT YOU BELIEVE

THE PROBLEM OF TRUTH

"But Stan, I just don't see how you can believe that and be a sociologist," Andrew said as he sat back, sucked on his pipe, and blew yet another smoke ring into the air. It was an especially large ring this time, and it hung together nicely as it wafted its way toward the heavens. The quality of the smoke seemed a good match for Andrew's confident mood. "I mean, how many religious people do you see walking around these halls, anyway?"

It was a new twist on an old theme. From the moment I decided to go on to graduate school in sociology, I had encountered Christians who were perplexed about my decision. For one thing, many of them didn't know what sociology was. But they did know what it sounded like. And none of the rhymes seemed to them like a worthy pursuit for a Christian. Those who did have some exposure to sociology were often even more incredulous. They simply couldn't understand how a committed Christian could enter the field. Or would even want to.

Andrew wondered the same thing, but not because he was a Christian. Quite the opposite. Andrew was what I call a confident agnostic. He was, in other words, very sure of his skepticism. And he knew what he was talking about. Raised as a Roman Catholic and educated in Jesuit institutions, Andrew was well versed in church history and teaching. Indeed, he had moved to his agnostic position while still under the tutelage of Jesuit teachers. He had found Heidegger and Nietzsche more convincing than Augustine or Aquinas. And he was fairly confident that the truths of sociology had laid to waste a good portion of Christian thought.

"Granted, Andrew," I said. "There aren't a lot of religious people in our department. But that hardly seems relevant. There aren't a lot of religious people on this entire campus. This isn't exactly the hotbed of religion in America, after all."

"But that's precisely what I'm saying," continued Andrew. "You have here assembled some of the brightest minds in the nation. They have thought long and hard about life in all its complexity. And what have they concluded? That your God exists? Hardly. That your God is irrelevant is the more general conclusion—that if he exists, he doesn't seem to be particularly concerned about making himself known. Face it, Stan, the consensus among the world's brightest minds is that your God is an irrelevancy. A nonfunctioning being, if he is a being at all."

Without a doubt, Andrew was correct. The modern university, I had long since discovered, is pervaded by a secular atmosphere. It may not be true that all of its faculty are irreligious. But it was certainly the case that—if they are—they kept their religiosity to themselves. I knew of no faculty member who thought his or her faith important enough to bring up in the classroom. Indeed, the only faculty who talked about religion at all were those who brought it into question, the skeptics, in other words. Everyone else seemed to think it was entirely irrelevant to the intellectual quest.

"I'm sure you're right," I admitted, "but I'm not at all sure that it's very significant. A few years ago, the consensus on this or any other campus in the Western world would have been quite different. In fact, a hundred years ago or so, you couldn't have even secured a faculty position if you weren't a Christian. Times change. The consensus changes. God's being is not determined by popular opinion, my friend. What everyone believes on this campus or any other is an interesting fact, but it doesn't seem especially pertinent to this discussion."

CHAPTER 5

"Come, come, Old Man," Andrew intervened with much enthusiasm. "You know what I mean. Western intellectuals have changed their minds on the issue of God precisely because the evidence has turned against him. In field after field, theological explanations have been replaced by empirical ones. Modern scholars didn't just decide one day not to believe in God. They decided, instead, to look at the evidence. And what they have discovered is that tornados and earthquakes are not acts of God, but acts of nature, the natural consequence of natural conditions. The issue is not so much that there is a growing consensus about God's irrelevancy, but why that consensus developed. And it developed because . . . well, because what you believe about God isn't credible to most thinkers these days."

"You're still doing it, Andrew," I said, this time with a bit more defensiveness than before. "You're still reasoning from popular opinion. Of course there are reasons why the consensus in the modern academy exists. But there were reasons—good ones, I have come to believe—why the consensus was very different not too many years ago. You say that modern thinkers have replaced theological answers with empirical ones. That's true, I suppose. But why in the world do they assume that there is any contradiction between theological and empirical answers? Why is it that they assume the tornado was caused *either* by God or by nature rather than both? There is certainly no logical reason why a God who is the Creator of the world could not be the cause behind the events of nature; in fact, that is precisely what most Western scientists assumed until the nineteenth century. So don't tell me that the empirical evidence is overwhelming. And don't tell me I have to believe what every other modern scholar believes either."

Andrew took his pipe out of his mouth and gave me a huge, gentle grin. "I hit a raw nerve on that one, didn't I?" He got up, pulled the trash can over by his chair and began tapping his pipe against the side of the can. "Look," he continued a bit more thoughtfully, "you're right about the empirical argument. That was a dumb one. And I suppose consensus doesn't prove anything either. But I do contend—and, in fact, am quite convinced—that what you believe about God is not particularly reasonable, especially not for someone trained in sociology."

He paused a bit more, while working on an especially obstinate piece of tobacco residue, and then looked me straight in the eye. "Look, Stan," Andrew said, pointing his pipe directly at my nose, "you're a sociologist of religion. You know better than I why people turn to religion. You know good and well that religion is sociologically predictable—that religion is in large part a function of where one is born, one's class, status, background, and so on. You put people in one set of circumstances, and they believe one thing; you put them in another, and they believe something quite different. It's as simple as that. Belief results from social conditions. Period. So how in the world can you sit there, knowing that, and still think your beliefs are true?"

Again, Andrew was correct. Religion, I knew, was socially transmitted, even the Christian faith. We learn our beliefs from others. And while Christians believe that such learning is superintended by God's Spirit, we also know that those who do not hear the Gospel, cannot know the Gospel. And, thus, the "knowing" seems highly contingent upon the existence of social conditions which allow the "knowing" to take place.

But for the first time in our discussion Andrew had made a serious tactical blunder. And I couldn't resist letting him know about it. "You know what you just said, Andy?" I muttered quietly. "You just told me that people believe because they live in the midst of social conditions that make their beliefs plausible; that what people believe depends on social conditions. So what does that tell you about the consensus in the modern academic community, the consensus that assumes that God doesn't exist or is irrelevant to the academic enterprise?"

Andrew was very bright and knew exactly what I was driving at. And so he did what all bright folk do when they're caught in their own argument, he kept quiet and hoped that I would talk my way into a blunder of my own—which was always

CHAPTER 5

a likely possibility in my case. But I thought he was listening, really listening, for the first time in our conversation. And so I decided to pursue the issue a bit more.

"What's good for the goose is good for the gander," I went on. "If I believe what I believe because of my social conditions, then you believe what you believe because of your social circumstances—and so does everyone else around here. And if that's the case, then let me turn the question back on you: How come you're so sure you are right? And why do you put so much stock in the fact that all these bright folk around here are agnostics? Maybe this is just one grand fellowship of error, a lot of very intelligent people who believe the same erroneous reasons for their very erroneous conclusions? If I'm in error for believing what others believe, why aren't you?"

A long silence ensued, much of it focusing on the relighting of Andrew's pipe and the nervous fidgeting of a pencil on my legal pad. In my mind, I replayed about a hundred different answers to my question, knowing that Andrew knew them all, and worrying that Andrew knew a hundred and one.

"Touché," Andrew finally said with a sturdy, considered voice. "Touché! But," and here the smile returned to his face, "you may have won the battle and lost the war on that one. My original point was simply that belief in God isn't a very reasonable thing for a sociologist. What you have just pointed out is that unbelief isn't particularly reasonable either, since it too is just the product of social circumstances. The point is, none of us have reason to believe anything. We are all the products of our environment. The most reasonable conclusion, under the circumstances, is that life is absurd and meaningless, not that life is the result of a Creator God or some such thing. So I think my original conclusion holds. And you have helped me prove my point."

As puffs of smoke now started pouring happily into the air, my spirit descended in sync. *Andrew was correct,* I thought to myself. I just shot myself in the foot. For although I had undermined the bases of his beliefs, hadn't I also undermined the bases for my own? And didn't that leave both of us in the position of having no bases for believing anything? I was about to admit my predicament, when a voice came booming over the partition.

". . . you'd be right, Andrew, except for two things. First, Gaede didn't say that beliefs are only the product of their social conditions. That was your claim, which he simply used against you. Secondly, if your own argument is correct, Andrew, then not only are all religious beliefs absurd, but beliefs of all kinds are absurd, including those which support science and sociology. For they too are supported by certain social conditions which make them believable."

The voice continued in clear, crisp tones. "In other words, Andrew, by your logic, the discipline you are studying is also a meaningless enterprise. What that suggests, interestingly enough, is that you have used sociology to show that all knowledge is absurd, including sociological knowledge. The question is, if sociology is absurd, then how can you have any confidence in the sociological reasoning which led you to your absurd conclusion in the first place? Your absurd conclusion is based on an absurd argument."

At this point, the voice became embodied as Dr. Timpkin came breezing around the corner. Andrew and I were sitting in his outer office, a large area set aside for books, research material, and graduate students—like me—who were assisting Dr. Timpkin with his teaching and research projects. The outer office was separated from Dr. Timpkin's personal office by a partition, an opaque piece of glass that did a good job of keeping people from seeing one another but very little, apparently, to obstruct sounds. For that reason, I rarely used the outer office when Dr. Timpkin was there. Indeed, until that very moment, I had assumed he wasn't there. Dr. Timpkin was on leave from the university, undergoing cancer treatment, and he hadn't been in his office for months. I was surprised he was up and around at all. But I was especially surprised to see him back in his office, looking fit as a fiddle and primed for verbal combat.

CHAPTER 5

"I'm sorry, Dr. Timpkin," I sputtered, ignoring his comments to Andrew, and trying to make up for a social faux pas. "I didn't know you were in today. Andrew and I can go somewhere else to chat."

"No need, Stan," he chirped in quickly. "No need at all. I've been enjoying your conversation immensely. Besides, I am tired of being cooped up at home. I just came in to my office to go through my mail and get a little exercise. Nothing important. No need to apologize."

A few awkward moments of silence followed, neither Andrew nor I knowing whether to restart our conversation or politely excuse ourselves. I knew, as well, that I should say something to Dr. Timpkin about his illness—at least ask him how he was feeling or tell him that he had been missed. But I'm not all that adept at handling such situations, especially not when it involves a superior. And so I did the only thing I could do, which was to sit there and look stupid, while this uncomfortable silence slowly consumed the entire office.

"So Andrew . . . ," Dr. Timpkin broke in, as he walked over to where we were sitting and propped himself up on the edge of my desk, "what do you think of my point? . . . And while you're thinking, take that silly stick out of your mouth, why don't you. Not good. Cancer you know. Bad disease. People have been known to die of it. . . . So, what's your comeback?"

Professor Timpkin was clearly back in form. A very bright man, and a superstar in the department, he was known for his direct style and energetic manner. He used words sparingly but with great effect. Most impressive to me, he was one of those rare individuals who was able to be frank and gentle at the same time, so that you always knew when he disagreed with you, but you never minded. In fact, it was almost as if he were doing you a favor by being direct, as if he were only telling you off because you were worth it to him. Behind his candor, in other words, there was warmth and affection.

For that reason, when he confronted Andrew about his

smoking and his logic, Andrew just grinned sheepishly and looked down at his pipe. He did the easy thing first, taking the pipe out of his mouth and knocking the excess tobacco into the trash can. By the time he had maneuvered his pipe into his back pocket, Andrew was ready to speak.

"Maybe it is absurd, Professor Timpkin. Maybe sociology, as well as this entire academic enterprise and the human condition in general, is one gigantic farce. Nonsense. Meaningless. And those of us who are trying to figure out its meaning are the biggest fools of all."

"Perhaps," Dr. Timpkin responded. "Perhaps. But it is an odd thing, is it not, that if it is so nonsensical you would have the good sense to figure that out? In other words," he continued, "don't we still have a problem here? Aren't you still using your reasoning to come to the conclusion that reason, and life itself, is absurd? And if that's the case, then how can you trust the reasoning that led you to that conclusion in the first place? In other words, your conclusion itself is highly suspect if your conclusion is correct.

"It seems to me, Andrew, that you want to have your proverbial cake and eat it too. On the one hand, you want to trust your mental faculties—to use them, live by them, and reason by them. On the other, you are using those same capacities to conclude that they are not trustworthy or worth living by. That seems odd to me. Indeed, it seems like a predicament of insurmountable proportions.

"Gaede, here, has an explanation for your predicament, don't you, Stan?" I looked up at Dr. Timpkin with all the confidence of a novice in a high-wire act, desperately hoping he wouldn't ask me to supply the explanation he assumed I had. "Gaede believes," he went on ("praise God from whom all blessings flow"), "that both your ability to reason and your conclusion that life is unreasonable and absurd can be accounted for.

"You think—and you think quite well, Andrew—because you were created by a Thinking Creator who created you in his image. In other words, God created you with the capacity to reason and reflect on your own existence. You are also a member of a fallen race, however. You and your ancestors are 'sinners,' in the words of the Tradition, and thus you are estranged from your Creator. In your separateness, you cast around for meaning but there is none to be found. That is because there is no meaning and purpose apart from the One who created you. And so, alas, you conclude that life itself is absurd. A farce. A charade. Well, that is exactly what you ought to conclude, from Gaede's perspective, if you're thinking straight. Because without the God of Reason, life should not be at all reasonable."

Dr. Timpkin turned his head in my direction. "Do I have it right, Stan?"

"Well, uh, of course . . . uh, that's, uh, exactly right. Couldn't have said it better myself," or something to that effect. Actually, I haven't the foggiest notion what I said, since I was absolutely flabbergasted by Dr. Timpkin's grasp of the argument.

"So. Nice to chat," he chimed in, breaking my incoherence with his words. "I've got to get going, I'm afraid. Doctor's orders. Can't be on my feet for too long." As he said this, he went back into his office and grabbed his briefcase.

In no time at all, he was back in the outer office, making a beeline for the door. "I'll tell you one thing, Andrew—it's good to be alive, my friend," he barked without even breaking stride. "Good to be alive!"

THE PROBLEM OF PRACTICE

Andrew and I sat there dumbfounded for a few minutes, trying to comprehend what had just taken place. Dr. Timpkin was a mountain of a figure in our department. To many graduate students—and indeed, many faculty—he walked on water. His work on organizations was considered by many to be not merely good, but absolutely top drawer. The best in the field. He was the reason many graduate students came to the university in the first place. And few who worked with him were disappointed. He was bright, affable, and extremely challenging.

One quality that had not been attributed to him, however, was religious. Not that he was irreligious certainly. Just that he never spoke about it or did anything that would make you think he had religious inclinations. Indeed, he didn't even seem particularly philosophical to me, at least not in the strong sense of that term. The questions that interested him were not, "What is truth?" or "What is the meaning of life?" but "How does a social organization work and why?" His mind was sharp but it seemed focused on details.

For that reason, then, I was absolutely astounded that Dr. Timpkin would even want to enter our conversation, much less do so with relish. And I was even more amazed at the philosophical and theological sophistication of his arguments.

CHAPTER 5

"What was that?" Andrew finally broke in. "What in the world was that!"

I laughed without thinking. "That, Andy my friend, was the utter demolition of your argument—top to bottom, side to side, inside and out, around and through, backward and . . ."

"No, no, no," Andrew responded, trying to ignore my rhetoric. "I mean, what was that theological argument all about? Do you think he really believes all that stuff about creation and sin? Or was he, as he put it, just restating your position—much better than you could ever do, I might add?"

I shrugged my shoulders, satisfied with the fact that the argument had been made and content as well with Andrew's conclusion about my lack of prowess as a debater.

"Do you know what the most significant thing he said was?" Andrew continued, apparently sidestepping his own question about Dr. Timpkin's intentions and moving instead to the content of his words. "It was that last line he gave me, as he walked out the door—'Good to be alive' he said. That's the thing that really sticks in my craw."

"Why do you say that, Andy?" I asked a little puzzled. "It was just a parting shot, wasn't it? A jovial way to say 'Goodbye'?"

"Maybe. But I don't think so. You'll remember that he said it to me, not to you. Besides, whether he meant it to be full of meaning or not, in point of fact it was a very pregnant comment, regardless of his intentions.

"You see, the problem with my position is not simply that it is self-defeating—as Dr. Timpkin so thoroughly and convincingly pointed out. The problem is that it can't account for 'the good' in life either. For if everything is absurd and meaningless, why do we keep having these life experiences that we can only describe as good? Why do I enjoy French cooking so much? Why do I love my wife with such a passion, and why is it so good to do so? Why am I exhilarated by a beautiful sunset or when I encounter spring? And why do tears come to my eyes whenever I see people sacrifice themselves for others?

THE PROBLEM OF PRACTICE

"And more impressive than any of these, consider Dr. Timpkin himself. The man has cancer, of a kind that is often fatal. My gosh, he's facing his own mortality in the prime of his life, at the peak of his career! Why isn't he shaking his fist at God? Why isn't he complaining about the injustice of it all? Why, indeed, is he affirming the goodness of life at a time when it doesn't seem particularly good, rationally speaking? The answer is that life is most precious when it is about to be taken away. But why is it precious if it's absurd? Why do we cling to it if it's meaningless?"

Andrew shrugged his shoulders, half in resignation, half in awe that something that heroic could be done. "To those questions Stan," Andrew continued after a breath or two, "I have no answers. And I am quite confident that Dr. Timpkin knew it."

Again, someone else had made a point on my behalf much better than I could have made it myself. But this one had greater poignancy to it, since it was a point that Andrew was making to himself. Under such conditions, I thought it wise to keep quiet. The less I talked, the better I sounded. And Andrew wasn't finished yet. "And you know what else, Stan," he began again, "I think genuine believers actually live better lives as well. Even when I'm in the depths of despair and life seems most meaningless to me, I am constantly struck by the fact that godly people live better lives. Indeed, maybe that's when it is most striking to me. Because when I see things for what they are—when I see life for the sham it is—I am reduced to a blithering idiot; I don't want to do anything, I see no purpose in studying, I am more than a little irritable, and I certainly have no time for others, including those like my wife whom I dearly love. Indeed, I can't give myself to others. There isn't anything to give.

"Those blind to the reality I see, however—those who live as if life is meaningful, who believe in a God who cares for them and loves them—they seem to enjoy life the most. In their ignorance, they go around seeing purpose and direction in everything and everyone. I find it absolutely maddening! I want to go up to them and shake them out of their stupidity, to say, 'This

117

is the world. It's absurd. It doesn't make sense. How can you be so content?' Sometimes I almost feel compelled to be a missionary for meaninglessness, an evangelist for absurdity. Because believers drive me crazy.

"And yet, they drive me crazy precisely because they live so well. And not just within themselves, either. It isn't just that believers are personally happier. I think, on the whole, they are even better citizens. That they treat others better. That they are more likely to care about their neighbor. When I'm feeling hopeless, how do I behave? Like a lonely, frightened child, trying to find my way and totally self-consumed. It is only when you have confidence that 'things are okay,' that 'God is in his heaven,' that you can go out there and confront troubles and help the needy. It's much easier to give of yourself if you think your self is securely in God's hands. . . ."

"Wait a second," I finally said, my incredulity having reached an uncontainable level. Though I obviously agreed with Andrew's position, it seemed to me that his line of reasoning ignored some important facts—facts that had given me trouble since my early years in college. "I'm sure it's true, Andy, that some believers—and I'm talking of Christians now—that some Christians do behave more lovingly because of their faith. But it also seems to me that sometimes their faith leads them in the opposite direction, that it leads them to ignore the needs of others.

"Take Marx's point about religion, for example. Now, you know I'm not nearly as enthusiastic about Marxist social philosophy as you are. But I do think he makes a valid point about religious people. The line we always remember, of course, is that "religion is the opiate of the people," meaning that it is a drug that helps the oppressed peoples of the earth endure their oppression. In some sense, Andy, it seems to me that's similar to what you're saying—that religious people feel better about things because they are not really seeing the world the way it actually is.

"But note Marx's conclusion. His conclusion is that religion is therefore a problem because it inhibits people from taking the action necessary to change their conditions for the better. In other words, religious people endure oppression when they ought to be throwing off the yoke of their oppressors. They put up with injustice rather than changing things to bring about more justice. They allow themselves and others to wallow in misery because their religion says, 'Everything will turn out okay in the end; wait till heaven; all will be well.' So in that sense, Christians may not be good neighbors at all. They may be the ones who are preventing positive change from taking place."

"Ah, Marx is full of crap on that one," Andrew blurted out impatiently. "Oh, he may be right that sometimes religion has functioned that way in history—that it has sided with oppressors rather than the oppressed. But in my experience, that is not how it usually functions in people's lives.

"The most sincere Christians I've known, Stan, were the Jesuit teachers at my prep school. They had a confidence about their faith that I've rarely seen. They were the most self-sacrificing, generous people I've ever encountered. I was an obnoxious student, you know. I asked embarrassing questions, bucked authority, and generally made an ass of myself. Yet these guys never flinched. They poured themselves into me, giving me hours of their time, putting up with my attitude problem, and encouraging me to take my studies seriously.

"And I think there's a relationship between their faith and their actions toward me. These guys were secure. They had confidence that they were serving God, as priests and teachers. As a result, they were able to transcend self-interest in a way I have not. Why? Because, from my perspective, I'm all I've got. I have to look out for myself because I'm the only reality I know or believe in. My teachers, however, got beyond themselves precisely because they believed that there was something more important than themselves. They believed—no, they knew—there was a God. And they found meaning and purpose in him.

"So I just don't see that Marx's point is borne out in actual fact. Certainly, political leaders sometimes use religion as Marx described. But the unwashed masses? The regular people? They seem to be energized by it, not mollified. If anything, religion in the hands of the people is dangerous. It leads to revolutions. Demands for change. What it doesn't lead to is passivity."

"Well, maybe," I said unconvinced. "Sometimes, certainly. But I still can't get that picture out of my head: of the Christian down on his knees in the midst of a fire storm, praying that God would put the fire out while the fire burns unabated all around him. Isn't there some truth in that image? Aren't some people so heavenly minded that they are of no earthly good? Don't Christians often use God's sovereignty and providence as an excuse for nonaction, for leaving things as they are rather than pitching in and bringing about change?"

"Of course," Andy shot back. "So what? People are people. And Christians are still people, making some of the same bad choices that other people make, and covering them up with religious language.

"But I think you're missing the point," he continued. "I'm not talking about people who use religion to serve their own self-interest. I'm talking about genuine Christians, with a deep faith in God and a love and devotion for him. I'm talking about the relationship between *real* faith and action. And, again, it seems to me that people with a deep love for God are anything but pussyfooters and pious pontificators.

"Your man who is down on his knees while a fire rages all around him—is that what Jesus would do? Is that what any of his disciples would have done? Is that what you would do? Of course not. That is certainly not what my Jesuit teachers did when they saw the fire storm that I was living in when I came to their school. They rolled up their sleeves and started punching me into shape. The person who ignores the needs of others so he can pray is thinking about himself, not his God. Besides, I have never understood that metaphor anyway since I see no reason why someone can't pray and fight a fire at the same time. Stupid."

We sat there for a little while, Andrew having finally vented his spleen and I having finally become convinced of my own position. As the silence began drawing out for an uncomfortably long time, Andrew once again drew out his pipe from his back pocket. I watched him begin the process of relighting his torch— knocking out the old grime, piercing the mouthpiece with a pipe cleaner, stuffing just the right amount of tobacco in the bowl, and pressing it down with a series of gentle but firm thumb strokes. Finally, it was ready for the match, and with a swift upbeat of his hand, the fire ignited and the pipe began having its desired effect. Once again, Andrew was blowing smoke rings.

"Andy," I finally said, jumping back into my earlier role, but feeling much more like a doctor now than a lawyer, "if you believe what you're telling me, then why aren't you a believer? If the best people you have seen were your Jesuit teachers, then why don't you want to be like them? If the people who get the most out of life are those whose lives are centered in God, then why haven't you located yourself there as well? What's holding you back?"

"Ah, ha," Andrew smiled, "now you're the evangelist. Having gotten me to state your own position, you want me to make it my own. You Christians are sneakier than I thought."

"Not true, Andy," I said, feeling a bit hurt. "Not true at all. I couldn't have made the argument you just made, not in a thousand years. I'm not even sure I believed it until a few minutes ago. For me, being a Christian doesn't have so much to do with its effect, but its truth. I believe Jesus really is the Christ. I know I'm a lost soul without the forgiveness that he offers me. I come to Christ because I need him and he is the only one who can satisfy my need. Sounds selfish, doesn't it?"

"Nope," came Andrew's quick response. "Sounds fine to me. Only those who recognize their need for God can have that need fulfilled. And it is precisely those who find such fulfillment, that will then be freed up to be the loving Christians I admire."

"So, then, what's the answer to my question, Andy? Why haven't you taken the plunge yourself?" As I spoke a couple of professors walked by our door, talking excitedly about a joint research project, totally impervious to the fact that they were intruding on our conversation. Their voices soon passed, but Andy kept his eyes glued on the door. Eventually, he took his pipe out of his mouth and used it to point to the door.

"That's the reason I can't take the plunge, Stan. Those people out there. They are my ambition. They are the ones I aspire to be like someday. They are holding the positions I want. They are the ones I admire. And Stan, not a one of them believes what you believe." His voice trailed off, as if his conclusion was one he only reached reluctantly.

"But what difference does that make?" I implored. "You don't have to be like them to be one of them. You can have an academic career without emulating their philosophy of life. That's my intention, after all. I'm not planning to trade in my faith for a degree. I think it's possible to have both. At least, it had better be possible or I'm in trouble."

Andrew looked at me, as if to affirm the fact that I was in trouble. I ignored his gaze.

"You don't understand, Stan. I'm not interested in becoming a carbon copy of them. The problem is, those folks—and their colleagues in the modern academy around the world—are the brightest people I know. It isn't just that I respect them, I respect their opinions. By and large, their very considered opinion is that your God is not a particularly reasonable thing to believe in. I've read their books. I've listened to their arguments. And I cannot disagree with their conclusions. You see, Stan, I'm a lot like you. The issue for me isn't what I would like to be true, but what is true. Your quest for truth has led you to Christ. Mine has turned me in another direction."

"But, Andy, what about your Jesuit teachers?" I pleaded. "Those were pretty bright folks, were they not? They believed in God, as you so forcefully argued a few moments ago, and it had a radical impact upon the way they lived. Why can't they become your model for belief as well as life?"

"Oh, I suppose that's possible," Andrew sighed. "But those

were the guys that introduced me to modern thought in the first place. They opened up the books that raised the crucial questions. And by and large, I didn't see that they had any answers. I guess, to some extent, they answered my questions with their lives rather than their words. But I need words, Stan. I am a man of words. I live by them, make my way by them, earn my place through them. I need answers to the questions of the modern academy."

I sighed heavily at that one. "I guess I don't really believe that, Andy," I finally confessed. "There are words—ancient as well as modern—that deal with your questions. It seems to me that Socrates raised your questions repeatedly. And what about Solomon, for heaven's sake? Ecclesiastes is precisely about the meaninglessness you describe. And the last two centuries are full of men and women who have struggled with your questions and become people of faith—Kierkegaard, Bonhoeffer, Niebuhr, and Lewis to name just a few. I don't agree with all their conclusions. But these folks were not satisfied with facile answers. And they were men of words, as you say. Why don't you find their words helpful? Why aren't they the ones you look to for assistance?"

"They're not sociologists, I guess . . . ," Andrew said, almost flippantly. And then, catching himself, "No, that's not it. That's dumb. It's more than that. . . . Look, the thing is, they're not walking around in those halls out there, Stan. They are not flesh and blood to me. They are not the ones I have to deal with in the classroom every day. They are not the profs I admire, who walk through these corridors so excited about their research that they can't keep their voices down. What I'm saying is that they are not part of my daily experience, and for that reason, their words aren't all that helpful to me right now."

More silence ensued and Andrew started working on his pipe again, this time trying to get the fire reengaged without relighting it. "Well, Andrew," I finally broke in, "you know we're back where we began a few hours ago. Whether you'll admit it or not, you're still arguing from consensus. You're still saying that you can't bring yourself to believe something that all these bright people out there don't believe. You've given it an existential twist, I suppose. And you've talked about it as a search for truth. But the bottom line is, those profs out there are functioning as an authority in your life. And right now, they hold the privileged position of defining truth for you. Isn't that right?"

Andrew looked at his watch without answering my question. "I've got to get home, Stan," he said. And then looking down at the pipe he held in his hand, "I've also got to change tobaccos or something. This stuff rots." He banged the pipe extra hard on the side of the trash can and roughly stuck it in his pocket.

"Maybe it's the pipe," he said as he got up out of his chair, gathered up his books and made his way for the door. "I don't know what it is, but something's wrong. It just doesn't have the flavor it used to have." He paused at the door. "You comin'?"

"Naaa," I whined as I pointed to the pile of books on my desk. "I've got to stay and finish this paper on Comte. What a complete bozo that guy was. 'The Father of Sociology,' this book says. Yuk. It's embarrassing to have a parent like that, you know? This discipline definitely needs a different ancestry."

I wasn't saying anything worth listening to, so Andrew didn't. He just looked back at me with his half-cocked smile and said, "Goin' it alone again, huh Gaede?"

From his tone, I knew exactly what he meant. And it had nothing to do with Comte, my paper, or even staying in the office. But though Andrew meant it as a compliment, it seemed to me that he had it wrong. Quite wrong.

"No sir, Andy," I replied. "That's the one thing I don't have to do."

Andrew looked down at the floor and then opened his grin just a bit wider. And slipped quietly out the door.

PRACTICING THE TRUTH

Over the next few months, Andrew and I had many more conversations about religion and life, but nothing quite so personal as that day in Dr. Timpkin's office. For one thing, Andrew never again argued the case for belief. If we got into a discussion of religion, he was adamant in defense of his own position, as was I. But for another, most of our discussions were dispassionately biographical—he would inquire into my religious background and I would ask him about his—and on the whole we seemed like two social scientists more interested in figuring one another out than in pursuing truth. Which, in fact, was the case.

Into this circus of voyeurism there was one important interlude, however. And once more it was precipitated by Dr. Timpkin. Again, it happened in Dr. Timpkin's outer office. Again, it was seasoned with a professorial conversation. But this time, the professor doing the talking was not Dr. Timpkin himself, but one of his colleagues. Indeed, though Dr. Timpkin was the focus of the conversation, he wasn't doing any talking at all. For the event that caused all the commotion was nothing less than his memorial service.

"I can't believe he said that," intoned Professor Swinkle. "The gall of that man, to lecture us like that! As if he could tell us something we didn't already know."

CHAPTER 5

The "man" giving Dr. Swinkle heartburn was not Dr. Timpkin but the pastor who had delivered the message at Dr. Timpkin's memorial service. From what I could gather—and this was all based on hearsay since I was unable to attend—the man in charge of the service had been Dr. Timpkin's pastor. He was apparently on the youngish side but otherwise a fairly typical cleric. That meant that he worked with regular people and did the things that regular pastors do. And most importantly to Dr. Swinkle, it meant that he had a regular college and seminary education and certainly not the years of education and scholarly expertise acquired by Professor Swinkle and his colleagues.

"I find it extraordinary," chimed in Dr. Fenstin, "that people continue to believe that sort of dribble. But I find it absolutely unbelievable that that man would attempt to dish out such beliefs on this campus. He was preaching in the University Chapel, after all! Out of respect for that institution alone, one would think he would keep his beliefs to himself."

"It was Timpkin's memorial," Dr. Brinkley piped in. "I didn't particularly agree with what was said but, from what I understand, the fellow simply gave the sermon he was asked to give by Timpkin himself."

"I don't believe that—I don't believe that for a second," retorted Dr. Swinkle. "Timpkin was a superb intellect. I understand he was also a regular churchgoer but he never let that interfere with his thinking—or his sociology. I think that pastor just thought he had a captive audience full of depraved intellectuals, and so he decided to tell us we were all going to hell."

"Oh come off it, Swinkle," continued Brinkley, "that was a well-planned message. He knew exactly what he was saying. And it looked to me as if Mrs. Timpkin agreed with every word he said."

"Hell's bells, Brinkley, don't you defend that rot," Dr. Swinkle bristled. "That was dangerous stuff he was spewing out, you know. That's the stuff that causes people to think that justice is in God's hands, rather than our own—that leaves people with

126

pie in the sky and misery on earth. It's that sort of thing that makes progress so bloomin' difficult in this country. People that should be marching in the streets are down on their knees instead, worrying about saving their own souls rather than the soul of a nation. Dangerous stuff, Brinkley. Dangerous stuff."

"And pretty damn stupid," chimed in Dr. Fenstin. "I still can't believe he would give that sermon here. To us, of all people. In that audience were some of the best minds at this university. To subject them to that drivel is absolutely vulgar. Pornographic, if you ask me. The dean's going to hear about this, I can tell you that. I shall not tolerate that kind of asinine behavior on this campus."

The conversation went on like that for some time, Dr. Brinkley weakly defending the right of the preacher to say what he liked and everyone else insisting that he had no right whatsoever to bring his barbaric religion before such an august body of thinkers. But on one thing all parties agreed. What the preacher said was ludicrous at best, the hysterical machinations of an untutored mind.

I found the whole scene chilling. From what I could gather, the preacher at Timpkin's memorial service had simply laid out the standard beliefs of basic Christianity. His delivery had not been erudite but the content was orthodox. And while some might say that a few of his points were a bit too sharp (for instance, "Dr. Timpkin will be in heaven and many of you will not"), on the whole, the tone was neither acerbic nor provocative. It was, in other words, mere Christianity. And I was a mere Christian. And it was not hard for me to imagine my fate if those same said professors discovered the depths of my convictions.

"Well," Andrew finally piped up after the rage of the professorate had cleared the hall, "that certainly was revealing, wasn't it?"

"Yeah," I followed quickly, "I'd better keep my yap shut if I want to get out of this place alive."

CHAPTER 5

Andrew laughed. "Oh, I shouldn't worry Gaede. Your advisor wasn't out there, after all. He appears sympathetic. Besides, these folks seem to think everything you write is made of gold. No, I'm talking about our conversation of a few months ago, do you remember? That's the one where Timpkin took me to task for my self-refuting argument about beliefs?"

"Yup, I remember," I said without thinking. "What about it?"

"Well, I came away from that conversation with two very troubling questions, questions I have pondered over and over again ever since. The first was about Professor Timpkin himself. I kept thinking about his Christian explanation of my predicament and wondering whether or not he really believed it. Well, I think we finally got our answer—"

"And?" I butted in impatiently.

"Well, obviously, he did."

"How can you be so sure?" I asked. "All we know is that his pastor put together a fairly annoying message at his memorial service. How do you know what Dr. Timpkin believed?"

"Oh, don't be so naïve, Stan. Those guys aren't just annoyed because of the service. They're annoyed because it was given on behalf of one of their most admired colleagues. They know good and well it was a message from Timpkin to them via his priest. That's what makes them so angry."

"Uh, 'pastor,'" I corrected. "But I still don't see how you can be so sure. Professor Swinkle seemed pretty confident that Dr. Timpkin didn't have anything to do with it."

"Swinkle, Ol' Boy," Andrew cocked his head as if talking to the hall, "'methinks thou dost protest too much.' Besides, Dr. Timpkin's death was no surprise. He has known he was dying for months now. He was one of the most organized people I have ever encountered. The idea of his leaving his own memorial service up to chance is inconceivable to me. Oh no. He knew, all right. And today he finally let his colleagues have it right between the eyes. Whamo!"

"Okay, okay," I cut him off, not wholly comfortable with the combat metaphor. "Let's assume he was a Christian. What difference does that make to you? And what was the other question you had answered, by the way? The date of the Second Coming perhaps? Or was it something more grand?"

"Hey, you really are a little edgy today, aren't you?" Andrew laughed. "Look, you're just a graduate student, Stan. A nobody, remember? They're not going to be after your scalp if you're a bit religious. Don't go zealous on them or anything like that, and you'll be okay."

Andrew laughed a few more times and then became suddenly serious. "What difference does it make? I'm not quite sure. Yet, anyway. So let me take the second question. It came from you, by the way. At least indirectly. Actually, what you did was accuse me of being a follower, if you'll remember. In so many words, you said that I was a skeptic because most modern scholars were skeptics, the implication being that I was more interested in following the modern crowd than discovering truth.

"That implication is wrong, by the way. I am very much interested in truth, Stan. But I had to agree with you that my search for truth has been substantially guided by modern thinkers and scholars. I'm not going to apologize for that, however, since I happen to believe some fairly substantial scholarship has occurred in the modern era—you do too or you wouldn't be pursuing a Ph.D. in sociology at a university like this. So I plead guilty to being impressed and swayed by modern thought.

"But here's the clinker: Modern thought, by its own admission, is pretty much in shambles on the question of ultimate truth. Metaphysics is the black hole of modern philosophy. And the social sciences, for all their contributions, seem almost inevitably to turn human beings into machines, or protoplasm, or worse. And so it seems to me that, on the basis of modern thought, I have to conclude some things about life that I don't want to conclude—like its absolute and total meaninglessness, for starters.

CHAPTER 5

"Now, when you reach those kinds of conclusions, you've got to ask yourself some pretty basic questions, not the least of which is, If modern thought leads down such a difficult path, why do I follow it? According to you—and I think you're probably right here—it's because the modern academy is dominated by such thinking and I am persuaded by the inhabitants of the modern academy. But that raises another question, which is the one that has bothered me ever since we last talked: Why is there such a consensus in the modern university on these issues? And why is it that skepticism is so rampant in the scholarly community today?

"What I have assumed in the past is that modern scholars are simply honest truthbrokers—people seeking to know the facts and coming to conclusions because that is where the facts lead them. What you and I have just witnessed today, however, throws that assumption into question, doesn't it? Because what those fellows in the hall were persuaded by is not the facts but their own egos, which are much too large to even entertain the idea that they might actually learn something from someone as common as the local parish priest."

"Uuh, 'pastor,' Andy," I quipped again. " 'Pastor.' "

"Whatever. Now obviously, everyone in the modern university doesn't have ego problems. But I think it's possible that most academics share the assumption of our hallway professors that the common people—like our priest at the memorial service—" (*I give up,* I thought.) "—don't have anything to teach them. What that means is that the modern academic community has decided, right from the start, whose facts to believe and whose not to believe. Religious people like our priest here, as well as their traditions, books, and insights, are not credible sources of information so their facts are dismissed. Other people, however, who use certain methods and reside in certain educational institutions, are deemed to be legitimate information sources. Their facts are worth considering, in other words.

"Now, if this is true then an interesting thing has happened in the modern university. It has become a place where people only talk and listen to one another. That is, the modern scholar tends to think that the only credible sources of information are other scholars just like him- or herself. So if you're a modern scholar and you have a question or a problem of some kind, you do not ask the local priest about it, nor do you ask your grandmother, the Bible, or anything else. You ask another modern scholar, who uses his or her own grab bag of legitimate facts to supply you with an answer.

"All of this would be fine, I suppose, if one could convince oneself that the modern academy is the repository of all wisdom and knowledge. But if it isn't—if it has excluded some important pieces of information or dispensed with ancient truths that indeed are True—then the modern university would end up being a place where people are caught up in a perpetual circle of error. Where one half-truth is built upon another half-truth, and where the end result is anything but the truth the university says it is seeking. The sad thing, of course, is that no one in the academy would ever know their predicament because the knowledge they need to discover their error is unavailable to them. It has been excluded right from the start."

Andrew dropped his hands, which had been circling higher and higher with every point, but had finally reached peak altitude and had nowhere left to go. He let his shoulders droop. Slumped down in his chair. And then replaced his impassioned countenance with a huge grin and pointed his finger in my direction.

"The question is, Stan . . . am I right about this or not? If I am, then it pretty much explains my predicament, doesn't it? It certainly explains why the modern academy could be so loaded with information and yet so devoid of ultimate answers that are either meaningful or helpful or hopeful. It also explains why there is such a consensus in the university on certain questions and why people like me—who have been on a search for truth in the midst of it—seem inevitably to come to one set of conclusions and not another.

"And finally, I think it explains Dr. Timpkin's behavior as well. The question is, why would he be so quiet about his faith all these years and then finally let his colleagues have it—in such unadulterated form—right at his death? The answer, I surmise, is that he knew his faith ran counter to the consensus on this campus. I doubt he kept it hidden out of fear or insecurity—given his stature and all—but out of respect for the value of what he believed. 'Don't cast your pearls among swine' is the way One Person has said it. And my guess is he understood that his beliefs would not be appreciated. So, he kept quiet on the matter until the very end, leaving only a note at his passing, letting his colleagues know that he did not share their consensus—that, on this issue at least, he was not one of them. He washed his hands.

"But . . . ," and here Andrew raised his hands in quandary, "it's all conjecture, isn't it. Pure speculation. It's a theory that fits nicely with the facts, but I haven't any idea whatsoever whether or not it's true. But it does make you stop and think, doesn't it Gaede? It does make you stop and think. . . ."

And so it did. Indeed, because of that conversation with Andrew, I was never able to think the same way again. Not about the modern academy, certainly. For although Andrew's theory was obviously one-sided and no doubt pertained to some academic settings more than others, I also came to believe that it contained more than a grain of truth. And it was in pondering that kernel that my own mind was opened up to a whole new set of possibilities. Possibilities of an education that took more than modern thought into consideration. Possibilities of a sociology that was open to truths other than those deemed legitimate by the powers that be. Possibilities for my own life as a scholar that I had heretofore never imagined doable. Or worthwhile.

And what became of Andrew? Well, nearly twenty years have passed since those days in Dr. Timpkin's outer office, and Andrew's whereabouts are unknown to me. I heard a few years ago that he has a fine position at a major university. And that wouldn't surprise me in the least. He is a man of superb intellect and great academic skills. Wherever he is, however, I am confident that he is continuing to make people think. And I am confident as well that those people, like me, will be grateful.

Did Andrew ever come to accept his own conclusions? I can't say. The evangelist in me desperately hopes he did. I want Andrew to know the Christ, whose Truth gives substance to all truths and whose Peace surpasses all understanding. But I have no way of knowing.

Perhaps, however, that is as it should be. I came to Andrew with the assumption that I had something to offer him, that I possessed a truth he desperately needed. As it turns out, however, it was Andrew whom the Lord used to instruct me, helping me to understand the predicament of modern thought in ways I had not understood it before, and challenging me to sail in different waters, to set my course for another destination.

The Lord works in mysterious ways, that's for sure. Mysterious ways and grand. And that is reason enough to let salvation remain in the hands of the God who offers it. And be thankful to him for teaching me through those whom I had assumed I was teaching.

CHAPTER 6
DISCOVERING HOW TO LOVE

LOVING TOGETHER

While I was having fun discussions at the University, Judy was out in the real world slaving away in the labor force. That didn't seem to bother Judy—she being absolutely Swedish about work—but I did feel a bit guilty about it. She was pregnant, after all, and trying to hold down her first full-time job as a kindergarten teacher. I, on the other hand, had nothing to do but read, go to classes, write papers, and argue. It was not a fair distribution of responsibilities, but I tried to make the most of it. For example, when Judy got out of bed at the crack of dawn each morning to go to work, I always managed to wave good-bye.

Now that I think about it, I have to admit that Judy really put up with a lot in those days. Not that I'm a piece of cake in my present form, certainly, but during the first few years of our marriage I was anything but an equal-opportunity husband. In my own defense, I believe this had more to do with upbringing than nastiness. But that didn't change the fact that Judy was the one who did most of the cooking, washing, and cleaning around the house. I contributed periodically, when it dawned on me she needed help, but it didn't dawn all that often.

Part of the problem was that Judy is nearly religious about not complaining, and I am equally pious about not noticing. When Judy realizes that something needs to get done, she just jumps in and does it. If the task starts to get overwhelming, however, she doesn't yell, "Time out! Hey you, Bimbo-with-your-Beak-in-a-Book. I need help." Rather, she just digs in her heels and works a little harder. Unfortunately, this approach is usually successful, which means that she manages the task without me and I never even realize how unhelpful I have been.

But sometimes she is not successful, and then things become interesting. My first clue that there is a problem usually arrives in the form of a nonevent. Dinner doesn't happen, for example. Or I run out of underwear. Or I go to bed at night and Judy's not there. For most husbands, I'm sure all of these would be glaring neon signs warning of impending disaster. For me—especially during the first few years of our marriage—they were mere oddities. Strange phenomena in an otherwise well-run home.

I remember coming home to just such an oddity one evening during our first year of marriage. I arrived at our apartment around 6:00, late at that point in our career since we usually ate around 5:30. I was worried that dinner might be cold or burnt or whatever, and so I rushed to the kitchen to apologize. When I arrived, however, I was confronted not by a fuming spouse but a great volume of nothingness—no dinner, no wife, and no evidence of human activity at anytime during the last century. Just our kitchen, in quiet repose, inert as the Rock of Gibraltar.

Now, I am sure that most husbands would have been alarmed by this scene but I was merely relieved. For some reason—I did not know why—I had been spared the indignity of delaying dinner and that was enough for me. The fact that my wife was gone was unusual, certainly, an oddity without doubt. But her absence was the reason for my reprieve. How could I be upset by something that had been the cause of my pardon?

After an hour or so of her absence, however, my mood began to change. Again, you'd think that I would finally start worrying about my wife. But again, you'd be wrong. What changed was not the disposition of my heart but the mood of my stomach. And it was turning decidedly ugly. *Where in the world is my wife,* I thought. *It's 7:30, for heaven's sake. It's bad enough that I had to watch Huntley-Brinkley on an empty stomach. Am I going to have to start studying on one too?*

I moaned like this for a good thirty minutes or so, never once coming up with the idea of making dinner myself, or—even worse—never once entertaining the thought that Judy might be in trouble. In part, this was because time has always been a mystery to Judy. She has never worn a watch, nor has she managed her life by the clock. This gives her a certain advantage over the rest of the world, by the way: she has the benefit of not getting ulcers about keeping on schedule, plus she never has to wait for anyone else. When Judy arrives, the rest of the world is already there. I used to take this personally, assuming that when she was late she was being inconsiderate. I soon discovered, however, that her mother was the same way, and neither one of them would hurt a flea. So being late had nothing to do with meanness or anything like that. It was simply a genetic problem: the whole time portion of the brain just never developed.

So, anyway, my assumption—as I sat there on the couch, now trying to read George Homans on an empty stomach—was that Judy had once again lost track of time but, on this occasion, in a truly monumental way. Since we were newly married, moreover, I had not yet figured out the genetic problem, so I couldn't blame nature for my predicament. All I managed to do was lie there, fret about impending starvation, and grow increasingly distraught.

Eventually, the door opened and in came my good wife, happy as a clam, with a mountain of laundry in her hands. To anyone with half a brain, it would have been immediately obvious what Judy had been up to. And had I been able to use the full extent of my faculties, I could have put the laundry together with the fact that she had a major exam the next day, and figured out that she was under a lot of pressure.

Unfortunately, Judy has a naturally sunny disposition. So even though she was under all this pressure, not to mention laundry, she was still trying to make the most of it and walked into our house with a big smile on her face. The smile—though evidence of a marvelous personality—did not have a particularly salutary effect on me. I was worried about my stomach, remember, and had come to the conclusion that Judy had, once again, lost track of time. Her big smile and happy "Hello," then, were mere evidence that she had completely lost touch with reality and that all my suspicions were correct.

"Where in the world have you been?" I asked indignantly. "It's almost eight o'clock."

Judy ignored the self-righteous tone and acted as if the sun were still out. "Oh, I had tons of laundry to do so I thought I'd take my books to the laundromat and study while I washed the clothes. I got a lot done but I still have a few more chapters to read before I can start putting this stuff down to memory." She paused. "Is it really eight already?" she asked, completely impervious to all the natural indicators, including a setting sun, neon signs, and shrinking stomachs.

"Hon, it's pitch black out there and it has been for hours. Half of Santa Barbara is sleeping already and the other half is no doubt making whoopee," the town reputedly consisting of the newly wed and nearly dead. "Two people are doing neither of those things, however. One is reading books in a laundromat and the other is entering the final stages of malnutritional *pathologico anemia!*"

Judy did not laugh. Nor did she cry. Nor did she give me the verbal tongue lashing I so richly deserved. Instead, the sun finally set in Santa Barbara, along with the laundry, and Judy walked tight-lipped into the kitchen. For the next thirty minutes or so, neither of us said a word or changed our position. The laundry remained in a pile on the living room floor. I remained on the couch, trying to read about exchange theory on an empty stomach. And Judy remained in the kitchen, taking out her frustration on a Jello salad and a half dozen innocent eggs (you have never seen fluffier scrambled eggs than the ones she put together that night).

By the time Judy broke the silence with "Let's eat," all the ingredients were in place for a nuclear holocaust. This was so, not only because of what you already know about our situation, but for two more reasons as well. First—and this will be difficult to appreciate, I know—I was still feeling rather self-righteous about the whole evening. I was not sitting on the couch feeling guilty, as I should have been. I was steaming about how inconsiderate it was for Judy to have been studying and doing the laundry instead of fixing our dinner. So by the time I came to the table, I was quite convinced that I was the victim of a great injustice.

Secondly—and this will take a little more explaining—you need to have a sense of Judy's approach to cooking during the first year of our marriage. People are motivated by different things when they whip up a meal. Some focus on the main course, making sure above all that the main dish is properly prepared. Others focus more on the before and after, putting great effort into appetizers and desserts and what have you. Whatever the focus may be, there is general agreement that the primary object of the thing is to put together a meal that is at once delicious and nutritional.

Judy came to the cooking enterprise, however, with a rather different set of values. Taste and nutrition were fine in their place, she believed, but they were of minor moment compared to the aesthetic requirements of a repast. Of highest value to Judy wasn't the way a meal tasted but the way it looked, and that meant a colorful variety of foods on one's plate, enhanced by a nicely designed place setting and augmented by candles and various, sundry other accoutrements of a well-orchestrated meal.

Now, in the long run, this turned out to be a marvelous thing, because it meant our meals were both a culinary and aesthetic delight. In the long run. For the first few years, however, it meant that I was treated to some rather unusual food groupings, all of which inevitably looked beautiful but tasted . . . well, unusual.

Like this evening for example. In spite of the fact that Judy was no doubt questioning the legitimacy of her marriage vows during the entire time she was preparing dinner, she nevertheless set up a beautiful table arrangement, with blue candles, green place mats, and yellow daisies, all of which tied in grandly with the place setting and serving dishes. She must have decided on this arrangement before she came up with the meal, however, because she matched the flowers with scrambled eggs, the candles with a blue jello salad, and the place mats with spinach.

Now, I am not opposed to any one of these delicacies on their own—though I question the merits of blue jello salad—but the combination seemed rather hard to believe. As I got closer to the table, however, I was forced to believe it and began wondering how I was going to properly offer thanks for the meal. Saying grace under conditions of war is always a feat, but when you throw scrambled eggs and spinach into the mix, things become especially dicey. "Dear Lord, we thank you for the immense diversity of your creation, for the rich mixture of . . ."

As we wait for this lengthy prayer to end, there is one last slice of information that needs to be added to the menu. In contrast to Judy, I grew up in a family that was suspicious of any word that sounded remotely like "aesthetics," and certainly, we would not have assumed it had anything to do with eating. As far as food was concerned, we were only thinly disguised barbarians, approaching the table much like Attila the Hun approached warfare. I remember trying to time the end of grace perfectly—fork in hand and pork chops at 12:00 o'clock high—so that I could spear the biggest piece before my older brother laid claim to it.

You may be thinking that this doesn't sound particularly fair, especially as far as my brother was concerned. But you should know that he was my primary role model in this whole business. I remember one incident that was particularly instructive. We were having barbecued hamburgers that evening and I was working on my third burger. I remember laying the bun out on my plate and commencing to give it full dress honors, layering ketchup, pickles, onions, and tomatoes on one side, and mayonnaise, mustard, lettuce, and cheese on the other. This was a rather involved process for me, since I had to get everything on in the right order and convince everyone else around the table to pass me various condiments at just the right time. Eventually, however, I had everything in place and was ready to top off my creation with a hamburger patty.

As I looked at the hamburger plate, however, I noticed that there was only one patty left. My brother had noticed this fact as well—long before I did—and was patiently waiting for me to finish creating my sandwich. Precisely at the moment I realized there was only one patty left, and one second before I could grab it, my brother swept the lonesome patty from the plate and into his mouth, never to be seen again. As I sat there, contemplating my hamburgerless creation and my brother's satisfied smile, only one thought came to mind: "Never again. NEVER AGAIN."

So you can see that with that kind of conditioning I was not prepared for candles, coordinated place settings, and matching food groups. I was not prepared for much of anything except eating, and that was to be done in the fastest, most efficient way possible. This approach to eating, of course, assumed one important detail: that one would want to eat whatever had been placed on the table. That was an extremely salient matter, you see, because if the food wasn't appetizing, then there was no reason to even be at the table. One didn't come to dinner to talk or relax or enjoy time together. And one certainly didn't come to the table for aesthetic purposes. Gastronomics were the entirety of the matter, as far as I was concerned, and as I prayed for the meal that evening, I knew that the entirety of the matter was missing.

". . . in the name of the Father, the Son, and the Holy Ghost. Amen." I didn't usually end the blessing with an appeal to the Trinity, but if any meal required it, I knew this one did.

LOVING TOGETHER

When I opened my eyes, I was confronted again with the same spectacle, and I began contemplating my next move. One option was to simply begin eating. That seemed like the least appealing alternative, so I cast around for something to say.

"Uh, Hon," I inquired respectfully, "why is the jello salad blue?"

There was no answer.

"I mean," I continued, "I can appreciate the need for jello, and I even understand why your family insists on putting these little things in it, but . . . but . . . blue??"

As I looked over at Judy, I discovered that her eyes were fixed on me, now huge with disbelief and loaded with moisture, most of it by this time cascading down her cheeks and seasoning the spinach. I could tell that she wanted to say something—her lips were starting to quiver—but nothing would come out of her mouth. It did not escape me that, as far as my own well-being was concerned, that was probably a fortunate thing.

Tears speak louder than words, especially when they come from the person you love more than anyone else in the world. And as I sat there at the table, listening to the silence and watching Judy continue to improve the spinach, it finally occurred to me that perhaps I ought to be thinking about someone other than myself. Someone else in the family had needs, apparently, and just as apparently those needs were not currently being met. And with that realization, something rather dramatic took place. For the first time that evening, I finally began seeing things from Judy's perspective rather than my own. And suddenly, almost magically, nothing in the room looked quite the same.

The laundry, for instance, which had heretofore been nothing but an impediment to my appetite, suddenly turned into a form of service, something that Judy was doing on my behalf even though it might cost her a few points on tomorrow's exam. And the place setting, which prior to the tears had been nothing more than an unnecessary decoration, was instantly transformed into a love note, a way of telling me that this time together was special,

143

set apart, what the theologians call "holy." And the meal—that strange combination of blue and green and yellow, at its best— which had heretofore been merely unappetizing—was now an act of grace, a willingness to meet the needs of another human being even when that human being wasn't particularly worth meeting.

And me? Well, I had changed as well, for I had turned into a toad. A big, fat, ugly, warty old toad, mind you, whose primary contribution in life was to sit on someone else's lily pad and croak about the inadequacy of the accommodations.

Again I looked up at Judy, this time with my new perspective and this time with the determination to at least say something halfway civilized, if not altogether apologetic. But Judy's expression stopped me dead in my tracks. For this was not the face of someone who was waiting to hear another word from me, but of someone who had something she definitely wanted to say and had finally cranked up the chutzpah to say it. I bit my tongue and prepared for the worst, knowing that the worst was precisely what I deserved.

"Stan . . ." She hesitated. "Stan, I have a suggestion. Why don't you take your dinner and shove it" (uh, oh . . . it's fastball time) "right into the refrigerator. Let's just forget about dinner altogether tonight."

And before I could figure out what she was talking about, she was already putting her plan into action, grabbing my plate along with her own, and whisking them into the refrigerator. I sat there, transfixed and speechless, wondering what in the world was coming next, when she suddenly grabbed a square white box out of the pantry and placed it on the table in front of me.

"What do you say we just have dessert?" she said sitting back down, her eyes twinkling through the moisture and looking right through me. "I went to the bakery this afternoon and picked up a pie. It's lemon meringue—not exactly your favorite, I know, but," she said, as she added a huge grin to the sunrise in her eyes, "it'll look good with the daisies."

LOVING ONE ANOTHER

As I think about that evening in Santa Barbara and a few others like it during our first few years of marriage, I am struck by a number of things—Judy's stubborn love for me, for one thing, even when I wasn't very lovely. And for another, my own insensitivity to the needs of others, especially to the needs of a young wife who was going to college full time and trying to run a household to boot. And then, of course, there is simply the miracle that such a young woman would fall in love with such a man in the first place.

But perhaps the thing that hits me the hardest, at this point in my life anyway, is how much I have changed since those early days of our marriage. Certainly, I have not fully licked the problem of being self-absorbed. That problem seems to dog me no matter how much progress I make in other areas. But in one area of my life things have changed, and quite dramatically: I am without doubt a very different husband when it comes to things domestic. I help out with the meals. I often do the dishes. I take my turn at various household chores. And Judy and I pretty much share the responsibility of raising our children. In short, though Judy is still the most productive member of the team, we are in fact a team. We try to work together on the domestic front.

One of the more intriguing things about this change, however, is that it has occurred without a single word of

145

admonition or direction from Judy. I can't remember even one
time when Judy has sat me down and said, "Stan, you're a pimple
on the face of this household. You're obviously here, but as far as
anyone can tell, you make no positive contribution to the family
whatsoever. It's time to grow up." That she did not say. And yet,
today, the family complexion is much different. The pimple has all
but receded. And a husband has decided to join the family. Why?

Before I can answer that question, I need to make two
clarifying comments, the first having to do with my wife and the
second concerning the nature of true love.

To begin with, it is important for you to understand that my
wife is not a docile, cheap-grace kind of woman. She does not take
all of my ill-mannered behaviorisms lying down, nor does she
always turn the other cheek when I say something rude. In fact,
Judy has a very strong ego and a profound sense of right and
wrong. For that reason, she is not one to bend the rules for the
sake of convenience, nor does she find it particularly easy to give
in when she thinks she's right. On matters of justice and morality,
she is very stubborn.

I say this because it would be easy to read the story of the
lemon meringue pie and conclude, "Oh, Judy is just one of those
passive, acquiescent kinds of people; she came up with the dessert
idea because she's not capable of standing up for her rights." In
isolation from the rest of her life, I understand how someone
might come to that conclusion. But as one of those people who has
had the privilege of living with her for some time now, I know
that that conclusion has about as much credibility as Mussolini's
view of history.

In truth, Judy finds it very difficult to back down when she
knows she's right, and it doesn't really matter to her whether she's
in the presence of her husband or the king of Siam. She has a solid
backbone, and from my perspective, it is one of her most
endearing qualities. As a result, regardless of her optimistic
personality and her natural love of people, she stubbornly refuses

to sacrifice truth for the sake of friends or relationships. Certainly, she is not confrontational. And, just as certainly, she would far rather laugh with you than debate you (she doesn't like arguments at all). But she does not knuckle under either, regardless of whose knuckles are inflicting the pain. A pushover she is not.

Which only makes her response to me all the more amazing. Because given her strength of character and conviction, the easiest thing in the world for her to do would have been to tell me to "shove it" someplace other than the refrigerator—not in words perhaps, but in deeds and innuendo. But she did not do that. She fed me lemon meringue pie instead, precisely what I didn't deserve.

And that brings me to my second, somewhat more extended comment. For I think Judy's behavior that evening was one of the truest expressions of Christian love I have ever encountered. That may not be altogether obvious, so you'll forgive me if I take just a few moments to explain what I mean.

The question is, why do I call it a true expression of love? The answer, by the way, is not simply because Judy backed down. Nor is it for most of the other reasons that are typically offered when people try to explain the nature of Christian love—that love which Christ expects of us and which we, as his followers, seek to exhibit.

I don't know about you, but growing up I struggled with two contradictory views of Christian love. On the one hand, there was the image of Christ, the suffering servant, the one who suffered in silence at his own trial, commanded us to turn the other cheek, and not repay evil with evil. This was the Christ of the cross, and it seemed to leave no room whatsoever for retribution or justice or even fair play. It simply said, Christian love entails submission and submission is the highest virtue. Period. Those who wish to practice it, therefore, must learn the art of self-sacrifice and perseverance. They must learn how to practice submission.

On the other hand, I was also aware of the image of Christ

the executor of justice, whose deeds were anything but submissive, who talks about hell more persistently and graphically than anyone else in all of Scripture, and who rides through Revelation like a conquering hero. Here is a man with a passionate concern for justice—not in spite of his love, but because of it. It is a love which cannot passively endure the atrocities of evil, which fights for the oppressed and turns the powers of this world on their heads. This is the Christ who saves, who liberates, who triumphs over evil. This is the God of justice.

Growing up I found both of these images convincing because both seemed to have roots firmly planted in Scripture. Nevertheless, they seemed hopelessly contradictory as well, and I couldn't for the life of me figure out how to live according to both images at the same time. Consequently, I didn't. Instead, I found myself vacillating horrendously on this issue, on one Sunday feeling like a sacrificial lamb and, on the next, like Constantine on the warpath, ready to impale any evil thing that managed to get in my way.

I have come to believe that both images of love are problematic on their own, precisely because they reduce love to a single kind of expression, when the Bible—taken as a whole—seems not to be comfortable with such a reduction. In saying this, I know I am stepping on some toes. And if you disagree with me, you should take solace in the fact that I have quite often been wrong in my life. But it seems to me that just as God—who is described as Love in the Bible—expresses his love through acts of submission in some cases and acts of justice in others, so it is that Christians will discover that love cannot be confined to a single, behavioral expression.

Take Judy's response with the lemon meringue pie. Her action in this case, which we might define as an act of grace or submission, was also an act of love because it occurred within a context of justice. That is, Judy's decision to forget about dinner and go straight to the dessert, thereby not giving me the drubbing I deserved, only "worked" because both she and I knew exactly what I deserved. Another way of saying it is that submission is an effective expression of love when the one doing the submitting knows he has the power and the right to do otherwise. When it is voluntary and surprising, in other words.

By the same token, submission doesn't work very well—and, in fact, might be wholly inappropriate—when the one submitting is powerless in the first place and the agent of abuse is indifferent to his crime. A few years ago, for example, a young man came into my office and described the wonderful relationship he was having with a young woman on campus. He portrayed it in almost idyllic terms. The only problem was, when I talked with the young woman a few weeks later, I discovered that he was totally manipulating her, to the extent that she was compromising her moral standards at his behest. Why did she go along with it? Because she thought she would lose him if she didn't submit to his demands.

Submission, in such a situation, is not an expression of genuine love but a response to powerlessness. Though the young woman thought she was submitting for love, in fact she was fanning the flames of this young man's manipulative tendencies. For her, then, the exercise of power (by standing up for her rights or terminating the relationship) would have been a far more loving response, since it would have confronted this man with his problem. Unfortunately, as is often the case with the victim, she felt herself incapable of standing up to him. And thus the cycle of submission and abuse persisted.

What this suggests, then, is that submission is not always an expression of love. But just as certainly, neither is the desire for justice. Very often, in fact, the desire for justice is little more than a rationale for "getting my fair share" or seeing the powerful humbled. A wife comes home late one night, and a husband, who feels unfairly treated, cries out, "Where in the world have you been, anyway?" That is the cry of justice, but not love. Love would worry about the other person at least as much as it worried about itself, and it would be far less interested in fair play. At the least, love would resist coming to conclusions before all the facts

149

are in. But sometimes, love might even go beyond the facts, overlooking a mistake and ignoring the need for justice altogether. Because love does the unexpected. It offers lemon meringue pie when no one in the world would have thought it possible.

So what do we do with Jesus' command to turn the other cheek? And what of any one of a number of verses exhorting us to do justice? Are they not to be taken literally? Is their validity in question? And if not, then how do we obey them?

Well, I am a Neanderthal where Holy Scripture is concerned, so you know I assume its validity. But it seems to me that no part of Scripture stands alone, that every part derives meaning in the context of the whole. What that suggests is that biblical specifics must be understood in the light of overarching biblical truths. And one of the grandest of biblical truths is what the New Testament calls the royal law and the Old Testament defines as the foundation of its instruction: We are to love God above all, and our neighbor as ourselves.

The commands to submit and do justice, then, find their meaning in this larger command concerning love. Indeed, Jesus makes it very clear that the reason for submission is love, that both its purpose and motivation can be found only there. Love, then, doesn't exist to serve submission. Submission exists as an expression of love. When submission takes place out of power-lessness, therefore, or in response to manipulation or abuse, it is not serving its intended purpose. And divorced of its reason for being, it is a highly problematic form of behavior and one that often encourages injustice.

The question is, when should our love take the form of submission, and when will its focus be primarily the concern of justice? There is no easy, simple answer, obviously. I will make this comment, however. For the majority of us, submission is the more difficult action and, for that reason, ought to be the higher calling. For while justice can very easily be employed as a cover for self-interest, submission very rarely is. Consequently, I have found it useful to make submission the first-order response, qualified by the necessities of justice. I call this my "submit unless" principle, and it assumes that the natural response for the Christ follower ought to be submission. This, I believe, is clearly taught by Christ. If Jesus had his way with us, I suspect that it would be as natural for Christians to submit to one another as it is natural for those without Christ to dominate one another.

But sometimes submission turns out not to be the most loving response. We have already talked about one example of this, when submission only serves to encourage an exploitive relationship. But there are others as well. Certainly, submission has moral and ethical limits, and one ought to always obey God rather than others. But submission is also constrained by responsibility. It is one thing, for example, for me to submit to a slap on the cheek from my neighbor; it is quite another to allow that same neighbor to slap my child. For while the first case might be an act of love on my part, the second certainly would not. Indeed, love would require protective action on behalf of my child and a determination to see to it that such a thing doesn't happen again. Anything less would not be loving, either to my child or the neighbor. Indeed, anything less would only serve to undermine the reason for submission in the first place.

And the reason for submission? "See how they love one another." See how a young woman, tired and weary after a long day—and with more than enough chutzpah to dump a lemon meringue pie on her insensitive husband's head—serves it to him instead. See what the love of Christ can do for a woman. And for her man.

LIVING IN LOVE

Which gets us around to the changes that have taken place in my life over the last few years. The long-term effect of Judy's approach was to turn me into a far more involved family man and a far more helpful husband. The question is, why?

The reason human beings do anything, of course, is a profound mystery. Take it from a social scientist who has given much of his adult life to the study of the human condition: We do not know why human beings do most of the things they do. We find clues here and there. We see certain kinds of relationships more than others. We know that some types of behavior are destructive. But on the whole we don't know much and for that reason are continually surprised. Healthy people can emerge out of ghastly environments. And sickos can pop up in the most pristine settings. Human behavior remains a mystery.

That said, it does seem to me that the changes that occurred in my life were not mere accidents. I mean this not only in the sense that they took place within the context of God's gracious will. I mean, as well, that there were certain elements in the story that made the outcome more likely. Indeed, I would go so far as to say that had these elements been absent, the change would not have occurred at all.

The first element I've already mentioned but it bears repeating: Judy, I quickly discovered, was a powerful woman.

That wasn't my first impression, by the way. During the early part of our courtship, I wouldn't have thought Judy and power were even on speaking terms. She had an easygoing manner and a ready sense of humor, and seemed uninterested in getting her own way. Flexible, was more like it. Go with the flow.

I was quite the opposite. I wanted everything to come out as planned. When I designed a date, for example, it was important to me that events proceeded on schedule. If the objective was to be at Taco Bell by ten in the evening, then I wanted to be standing in line by 9:55. Traffic congestion, long lines, car problems, and the like would drive me nuts. Because surely the sky would fall in if I wasn't digesting a burrito by 10:05.

Judy, on the other hand, could arrive at midnight and not bat an eye. In fact, I discovered to my horror—and this will knock your socks off—that Judy could give up on Taco Bell altogether and not mind in the least. I mean, we would drive up to Taco Bell and the line would be stretched into the parking lot. Naturally, I would handle this revelation with all the decorum of an orangutan, blaming Santa Barbara, Taco Bell, and the entire human race for this cosmic interruption. But not Judy. She would just smile and say, "We can wait." Or "Let's take a drive and come back in an hour or so." Or most incredibly, "Why don't we try Foster's Freeze down the road?"

Foster's Freeze? Give up on Taco Bell for Foster's Freeze? The mere thought nearly sent me into convulsions. I would rather have endured thirty-nine lashes. Foster's idea of salsa was shredded lettuce. Even if they had imported their sauces directly from Mexico City, I wouldn't have gone there. It was not on the schedule, not part of the plan, not on the agenda.

Anyway, you get the picture. For me, it was the same old story, wanting what I wanted when I wanted it. But for Judy, that was never the case. She was always more adaptable than I, always capable of delaying gratification, always willing to reshuffle the schedule. And so I naturally assumed that she had little use for power and, in fact, probably didn't even know how to employ it.

CHAPTER 6

Boy, was I wrong. For one thing, I discovered that when it came to matters of justice or ethics, she could be as stubborn as a mule. If the issue was Taco Bell, she was infinitely malleable. But if I went zipping past a little old man with a flat tire, she turned into blue steel. First came the subtle hint ("Stan . . . don't you think that man needed help? You know who I mean, the one with a cane in one hand and a spare tire in the other, who looked like he had an arthritic condition and was going on 120? Don't you suppose he could use some assistance?"). Second came the subtle manner (craning her neck to get a look at the fellow as we zoomed past and then adjusting every rearview mirror in the car so she could keep him in her field of vision). And finally came the silence. Deafening, ear-splitting silence. Silence with enough energy in it to put any man in orbit, especially the man who was sitting next to her, desperately trying to get to Taco Bell by ten o'clock.

In time, I learned that Judy had more than the powers of resistance going for her. Her greatest power was of a positive sort, getting people to do things they weren't inclined to do. She does this, not by manipulation but by encouragement. The truth is, Judy sees the potential in people, not the present reality. It is definitely a gift because I can't for the life of me understand how it's even possible. I have a hard time seeing the potential in people even when it comes out. Judy seems to see it even when it's buried under forty-five layers of nauseating reality.

At times this makes her appear naïve.

Judy: "Oh, Stan. I think Matilda's a sweetheart, don't you?"

Stan: "No, actually, I think she's a prune."

Judy: "She is not. She loves animals, and she's always looking after her neighbor."

Stan: "That's because she hates human beings and loves to butt into other people's business."

Judy: "I don't think so, Stan. She's a little insecure, all right, but she really cares about people. I'll bet she'd love to get involved with the meals-for-the-homeless program at church. I think I'll give her a call."

And sure enough, a few weeks later, Matilda is down at church, whopping up huge portions of spaghetti for the homeless and having the time of her life. And this kind of thing happens over and over again. In the short run, Judy looks naïve and hopelessly unrealistic. But in the long run, it is often her version of reality that becomes the future, either because she sees potential when everyone else sees the facts—or by the sheer power of encouragement, she transforms the future into the potential she assumed was there all along. Either way, about one thing I have no doubt in the world: She is one smart, powerful woman.

Now the significance of Judy's power—as far as my transformation is concerned—is not simply that she managed to see potential in me. More important, from my perspective, was what it said about her willingness to tolerate my domestic stupidity in the first place. You see, when Judy submitted to my irresponsibility, she did so out of strength, not weakness. Like the old man who needed his tire changed, Judy could have changed my tire (so to speak) through subtle hints and ten-megaton silences. She didn't do that. Instead, she endured my ineptitude—and even fed me lemon meringue pie on occasion. I soon discovered that it was because she was willing to give up her own power, not simply give in to mine.

The second ingredient in my transformation was love, in particular Judy's love for me. I have mentioned before the miracle of Judy falling in love with me in the first place, and I shall not repeat that story here. But the important thing at this point is not that Judy loved me in some general, foundational sense, like the love that family members often have for one another. The significant thing is that Judy's submission on the domestic issue was specifically motivated by love.

We give in to people for a whole variety of reasons, don't we? Sometimes we pick up after a roommate simply because we can't stand a messy room and it's not worth the effort to try and get them to change; we'll have a new one next semester anyway.

CHAPTER 6

Sometimes we give in to others because we're afraid of them, or intimidated by them, or for a variety of reasons find it difficult to stand up to them. And sometimes we submit because we assume that submission is our proper role. Children obey their parents for that reason, as do employees obey employers, citizens obey rulers, and so on. In all of these situations, love may exist, but it is not the immediate motivation for submission. A child loves his parents but that is not usually the impetus for submission; self-interest is the more likely motivating factor.

What I discovered in Judy's case was that her submission was not for any of these reasons. This came home to me when I began to unravel her image of an ideal husband. She grew up in a family with fairly traditional values, but her experience of family was not traditional at all. This is because her father died of polio when she was only three (just months before the Salk vaccine was distributed) and her mother didn't remarry until Judy was sixteen. This meant that, in theory, she grew up without a father during her most formative years. In theory. In fact, she grew up with surrogate fathers all over the place, from uncles, to friends, to her older brother.

The most significant fact was that she grew up with an image of her real dad based in part upon what she remembered (she claims a phenomenal memory; I have trouble remembering puberty, she repeats conversations between her parents that she overheard in the womb), but substantially based upon what her mother told her. So Judy grew up with an ideal father because her dad was never there to do all of the dumb, embarrassing things that real dads do. Her dad only did the wonderful things that ideal fathers do, like throw their kids in the air, listen to them when they have problems, take them on adventures, and have nothing but smiles on their faces 90 percent of the time.

One of the ideal things her father did, of course, was to help out a great deal around the house. He was particularly good at fixing things, I understand, but he loved to play with the kids, help out with the chores, and generally just be a peach of a guy

156

almost all of the time. I'm sounding sarcastic, I know, but there is strong evidence that he really was a great chap. Everyone says so. His pictures absolutely exude character and warmth. His brothers are all salt-of-the-earth folks. And his name was Stan, which I take to be strong evidence of nobility right from the start.

Unfortunately, "Stan" may be the only thing he and I had in common. I'm not such a peach of guy, and that was especially the case around the house. I grew up on a farm, and though it was a California farm, which sounds like a contradiction in terms, it was still a farm, and my dad was still a farmer. There was a fairly distinct separation of roles between husband and wife. Add to that the fact that my dad was not fond of domestic responsibilities and you come up with the picture of a father who spent most of his time involved in non-household endeavors. Make no mistake, my dad was a peach of a guy too. But his peachiness was not particularly evident on the domestic front.

What this means is that I grew up with one idea of a husband's responsibilities and Judy grew up with quite another. And what happens when two conflicting ideals collide? Well, most likely you get an explosion. Unless . . . unless at least one party decides to live with less than the ideal, which is exactly what Judy did. For when we got married, I immediately began acting like my father around the house (minus his peach). Judy, I think, was really quite surprised by this—and deeply disappointed—but she hardly even blinked. She simply hunkered down and did what needed doing around the house herself.

Now why did she do this? Well, for the first few weeks of our marriage, I suspect it was because she is not one to ask for help. As I've noted before, she is above all a doer. And in the beginning, I would guess that she simply thought it was more virtuous to work than complain. But that kind of virtue only operates for a certain period of time, especially when it runs headlong into a conflicting ideal, especially when the one with virtue also possesses power. So the question becomes, why did Judy submit to this arrangement—not for a few weeks or even months—but over the first few years of our marriage? In spite of her power? In spite of her ideal?

The answer, I believe, is that she loved me. I mean really loved me. And for that reason she was able to break through her own hurt and disappointment, and realize that my behavior was in part the consequence of what I had learned and observed. That I wasn't just a louse. That I was operating under a different set of rules. That, as problematic as those rules were for her, my intention was not to hurt her. And that, therefore, had she chosen to attack me for my behavior I probably would have taken it as an attack on my values, not to mention character.

What is it that allows us to understand those who disappoint us? It's not the natural thing to do, you know. I work every day with students, trying to get them to understand other people, other groups, other roles and relationships. One thing I discovered is that it's extremely difficult to get students to understand people who have hurt them. I remember, in particular, a missionary kid who had been the victim of discrimination growing up in a different culture. He was understanding of most cultures, but when it came to this particular one, he couldn't see past his disappointment. He simply refused to understand.

The one thing that allows us to understand in such conditions is love. Not because love is blind to hurt. Not because love ignores the reality of sin. But because love takes the focus off of self and sets it on the one who is loved. Love doesn't ignore, it overcomes. It overcomes the disappointment of a broken marital ideal and allows the one who is hurting to understand why the disappointment came about in the first place. Love produces understanding. And understanding, compassion. And compassion, forgiveness. Love allows a Man on a cross to look down at the ones who are crucifying him and say, "Forgive them Father, for they do not understand what they are doing."

And that's what Judy did during the first few years of our marriage. She had the power to come off the cross to which I was nailing her. But she gave it up. Why? Because she loved the one who was causing her all that pain. And so she did the most unnatural thing in the world. She tried to understand her husband.

And yet, that was not enough. At least, not enough to bring about the kind of transformation we're talking about here. And this is one of the hardest things for many Christians to accept. Power can be voluntarily restrained. A person might heroically turn the other cheek. But those factors in themselves do not precipitate a changed life. Life may continue to go around slapping people in the face.

While in college, I clearly remember a Sunday school teacher who was attempting to explain to us that Christians turn the other cheek in order to bring others to Christ. He said that the one thing people can't handle is nonretaliation. Indeed, they will be so surprised by it, he claimed, that they will want to know why you didn't retaliate. And then you will have the opportunity to share your testimony with them. Turning the other cheek, according to this teacher, was a wonderful means of evangelism.

When I heard him say this, I remember thinking, *Wow, that's powerful stuff*. One student in the back of class, however, was not so impressed, and before the teacher could even acknowledge his hand, he blurted out irreverently, "That's not true." He was slouching in his chair with his arms folded across his chest as he said this, looking as smug as a James Dean poster—and just about as compliant.

"I tried it as a kid," he remarked, acting as if he still wasn't. "I used to let other kids beat me up because my mom told me it was the Christian thing to do. And you know what? Not one kid ever came to know the Lord because of it. In fact, no one ever asked me why I did it, even though they knew I was a lot stronger than them. They just kept bullying me around."

He paused and then added with a smile, "Until one day I asked my pop why I had to let other kids bully me around. And Dad took me into another room so Mom couldn't hear us and told me that I had his permission to deck anyone who messed with me.

CHAPTER 6

Which I did. For the next week, I was laying kids out left and right. My mom had a cow, but it sure changed the way other kids treated me. In fact, some of the kids who bullied me around eventually became my friends. I made a lot more friends by decking people than I ever did by turning the other cheek."

At this we all laughed, everyone except the teacher that is. His face turned red, and he hurriedly tried to slough off James Dean's comments with some statement about, "You have to turn the other cheek with the right attitude." But everyone knew that the teacher had been bested. Common sense suggested that nonretaliation wouldn't always work. Common sense as well as the Bible. How many of those who nailed Jesus to the cross were transformed by his unwillingness to retaliate? A few soldiers perhaps. But not all. And certainly not the majority.

In point of fact my teacher was wrong. Jesus never told his followers to turn the other cheek to get a response. He told them to do it out of love for their enemies. He didn't promise them that their enemies would suddenly be transformed. He didn't reduce submission to an evangelism technique. Rather, he claimed that submission was a form of evidence. Evidence of a heart that was similar to his. Evidence of a true disciple of Christ. Evidence of Christ's love within us.

James Dean was practicing nonretaliation, not on the basis of love, but as a method of evangelism. And it didn't work—not for him, certainly, and not for those to whom he was submitting. As a technique, submission was a grand failure. But even if he had turned the other cheek out of love and Christian compassion, it may not have worked because people are not always impressed with Christian love. It seems dumb to some. It looks like an opportunity for others, especially those who are so intent upon getting their own way that they can't even appreciate the needs of others. They might view nonretaliation as a lucky break, a reprieve in the give and take of life, allowing them to take a little more than they gave for a change. The point is, submission alone will not transform lives. Submission, rather, results from a transformed life, a life transformed by the love of Christ.

And, thus, Judy didn't submit to my domestic habits in order to get me to change. She submitted because she loved me and, for that reason, understood why I was such an ignoramus around the house. That explains, too, why she was able to put up with this arrangement for more than a few weeks, more than a few months. You see, when techniques fail, we quickly discard them to find better ones. But Judy's submission was not a technique. And her actions were not based on the assumption that I would change. They were based on the fact that she loved me. And love is patient long after technique has fled the scene.

But I did change, nevertheless. And I changed for one simple reason. I loved her too. Which is the third and final ingredient of a transformed life. Out of love, a strong, powerful person quietly chose to submit to me. And out of love, I returned the favor.

You see, why does a person respond to an act of submission? There are, no doubt, many reasons, but there is one crucial factor above all else: The responder must understand it as an act of submission. When James Dean let his playmates bully him around on the playground, he got no response. Why? Because they didn't recognize his behavior as an act of submission. They saw it, instead, as an act of weakness. And so they weren't impressed at all. Indeed, they were repelled by his behavior. But once it becomes clear that someone is turning the other cheek voluntarily, in spite of their desire and ability to do otherwise, then it becomes a puzzling form of behavior. Something difficult to account for.

At the start of our marriage, I didn't view Judy's submission as submission. Nor did I view her behavior as weakness. I just assumed it was standard stuff, they way husbands and wives operate. That changed over time because I began to see things that didn't compute—primarily the way men operated in Judy's home. There men worked. Her new dad, whom Judy acquired at sixteen, did all kinds of things around the house, even though his occupation took twelve hours out of his day and Judy's mom was

CHAPTER 6

not employed outside the home. Judy's brothers also helped out. As it turns out, I did my share of chores as well. Because—as I discovered the first time I visited Judy—anyone who wanted to stay at the house for any length of time got a list of things to do. I definitely wanted to stay. So I worked.

At first, this seemed like a novelty, a strange little ritual that her family engaged in without rhyme or reason or importance. But it soon began to dawn on me that it was more than that. It was a philosophy of life. It said, "Everyone benefits from living here; so everyone contributes to the living." Though I would have enjoyed staying there without making any contribution at all, the philosophy said that wasn't fair. Not fair to those who are making the contribution on my behalf. Not fair to me, as well, because I deserved the privilege of serving as well as being served. And I had to admit, that made sense.

Once I admitted that, however, I had to face some serious questions. If it made sense in Judy's parents' home, why didn't it make sense in ours? Since both Judy and I had commitments outside the home, why was she the only one doing any work around the house? If Judy's dad wasn't a domestic freeloader, under his conditions, how could I be one under mine? That was the philosophical problem I was left with, and it was not easily resolved within my own set of assumptions.

But philosophy by itself is rarely persuasive, especially if you have grown up with different expectations, *especially* if the philosophy's implications are not in your own interest. What made the philosophy really hit home was when it finally dawned on me that this way of thinking was Judy's philosophy as well. "She grew up with this idea," I remember thinking one day. "What they do around this house is just as natural to her as what I grew up with around my own." And yet, what Judy and I were doing in our home was not in sync with her philosophy, but with mine. More specifically, Judy herself was adapting to my philosophy— even though it came at great personal cost and even though she didn't believe in it. She was doing it because she loved me.

That really hit me hard because it confronted me, for the first time, with the fact that her behavior was an act of submission. But so did something else. Not only did Judy have a different philosophy of household involvement, but I could tell she really liked her family's approach much better than mine. Not just theoretically but existentially. She enjoyed it. We'd go to her house for the weekend, and she'd love to get up on Saturday morning and help her brother with the washing or her dad and mom with breakfast. It made her feel good. It lifted her spirits. Indeed, I don't think Judy was ever any happier than when she was working with her family, talking and laughing and doing whatever it was that needed to be done.

And that, in the end, is what really unlocked my heart. Because I loved Judy. And when push came to shove (which means, when I could get beyond my own self-preoccupation), there was nothing in the world I wanted more than for Judy to be happy. I watched her function in her own family. I saw her pleasure in the give and take there. And I wanted that pleasure to be a part of our family as well.

So, I changed. Slowly, at first, because it wasn't easy. But more rapidly as time went along. Because it gave her pleasure. Because it was right. Because Judy had put up with what was wrong for my sake. And so it seemed a small matter, indeed, to do what was right for her's.

I love you, Hon.

CHAPTER 7
DISCOVERING CHURCH

WORSHIPING TOGETHER

Church is a problem. I don't know if you've ever noticed that before, but I came to a full realization of that fact during our stay at Preppie University. I did not notice it while growing up, that's for sure. Before I went off to college, church was not a problem. Church was church. It was there. You belonged to it. And that was the long and short of the matter.

But something happened to church about the time I left home. Church was no longer "there" for one thing. You had to go looking for it. But even when you found a church, it was still a problem. Either the preaching was a bit off. Or else the sanctuary was oddly shaped. Or perhaps the people were a bit off and oddly shaped. Indeed, the number of things that could be wrong with a church seemed to know no bounds.

This realization sort of took me by storm while we were at Preppie because it was there that we decided to commit ourselves to a local body of believers for the first time in our marriage. For three years we had resisted that commitment, in part because we hadn't lived in one spot for any length of time, but also because we were still living close to home. It was difficult to join a new church when your old church was only an hour or so away. Besides, regardless of what church we attended, there was always something wrong with it. We just never seemed to find a church that was right for us.

But when we arrived at Preppie, Judy and I covenanted together to find a church and stick with it. We were thousands of miles from home, after all. We needed friends. We needed fellowship. Most of all, we needed the nurture and care of the body of Christ. Preppie was a dry and barren land, as far as spiritual refreshment was concerned, and I knew that I was not going to flourish if I wasn't rooted in the good soil of Christian community. And, thus, finding a church was a high priority for us from the day we arrived.

At first, we thought we were in luck. The apartment we chose was located right across the road from Hillside Church, one of the larger evangelical churches in town. It was a beautiful church, urban in location but traditional in design. I used to love sitting on the couch by our front window because, regardless of what time of the year it was, I could always see remnants of Hillside Church peeking through the thicket of trees that danced in front of our apartment building. During autumn, as the trees undressed, the church seemed to grow in stature, becoming a bold brick edifice, daring winter on and challenging the world around it. Looking at that church in January, I knew why the gates of hell would not prevail against it. As spring arrived, the church relaxed. Flowers sprouted around its waist. The porch seemed to open up into a broad beamed smile. And the surrounding trees began to frolic again, in all their bright green glory, slowly covering the church with their progeny and, in the end, allowing me only a glimpse of the steeple's peak.

It was with excitement and anticipation, then, that Judy and I entered Hillside Church for the first time. The aesthetics were right. The church had a reputation for clear, biblical teaching. We had heard that they had a good program for college-age kids and young married couples. In short, from all we had seen and heard, this seemed like the perfect church for us. Convenient. Biblical. And beautiful.

Upon entering the sanctuary, we were not disappointed. The church was as lovely on the inside as it was on the out, elegantly

167

appointed with simple but distinguished lines. Sitting in the pews, you knew you were there to worship. No brazen colors to distract you. No gaudy fixtures to turn your attention from the One you came to enjoy. Just the presence of a well-crafted, well-maintained sanctuary, full of the quality you would expect from those who worship the Creator, and the reverence you need to join in the worship service.

And so we found it easy to worship there. We participated happily in the singing of God's praises. We were moved deeply by the reading of God's Word. We were encouraged mightily by the testimony of one of God's people, who had been saved at the brink of destruction by the God who loves to rescue the perishing. We had been edified and instructed by the preaching of God's servant, who had implored us to live a life worthy of our calling and worthy of the One who called us. And as I sat there waiting for the altar call—which I could tell was coming from the content of the last hymn—I was becoming ever more confident that we had finally found a church that we could call our own.

But then a most unexpected thing happened. As the pastor issued the invitation, he asked people to come forward—not to serve the risen Savior, not to repent, not to give one's life to Jesus, not to do any of the things that I had always assumed an invitation was designed for—but rather he invited us to come forward to join the church. Not THE Church, mind you, but his church. The Hillside Church. That big beautiful building that we were sitting in.

At first, I thought I had misunderstood him. After all, people use the word "church" quite loosely these days, sometimes referring to the church of Christ, sometimes referring to a local assembly, and sometimes referring to a building. I do it myself. But as the invitation droned on through the forty-fifth stanza of "Just As I Am," the pastor made it absolutely clear that I had not misunderstood.

"There are two ways you can join the church this morning," he said pleadingly. "First, you can come by letter of transfer if you are now a member of one of our sister churches. We'll do all the work for you, so don't worry about a thing. We'll take care of the details. All you have to do is come down these aisles and take the right hand of fellowship, and we'll accept you into our church with gladness and rejoicing.

"Others are welcome as well. And if you are not currently a member of one of our sister churches, then we offer you the waters of baptism. Come. Be baptized. And know the joy of being a part of this community. You need the fellowship of the church. You need us. And we need you. So, please, won't you come and join the Hillside Church? Won't you commit yourself to the work of this church?"

And the people came. By the score. So that by the time we had sung "without one plea" (to the innumerable pleas of the pastor) for the last time, the front of the church was pretty much packed. Everyone was clearly pleased with the response, especially the pastor. And he proceeded to welcome each of the respondents into the church, asking them their name and their mode of membership (letter or baptism), and then giving them the right hand of fellowship. When he was finished, he introduced the whole kit and caboodle as the newest members of Hillside Church, and asked the rest of the congregation to welcome them into the church with open arms.

Which I'm sure they did because this was one of the friendliest churches I have ever been to. We had a hard time extracting ourselves from the sanctuary, the people were so cordial, and in due time we found ourselves moving involuntarily into the young marrieds Sunday school classroom. That may seem like an unusual sequence of events, but if you've ever left a ball game with 100,000 other spectators, you'll know precisely how this worked. We were simply carried along by the crowd—except, in this case, the crowd was going to the Sunday school wing, not the parking lot, and the people were infinitely more jovial. Infinitely. I did manage to catch a glimpse of our apartment (a shelter in a time of storm) as we made our way through the front portico, but it was not to be. We were movin' in a whole different direction.

In no time at all, we found ourselves sitting in a Sunday school room, listening to a social chairman talk about future events and wondering how in the world we had gotten ourselves into this situation. In fact, I began to wonder if perhaps we had become members of the church involuntarily, against our will. Maybe walking through the portico evoked automatic membership privileges. Perhaps singing every stanza of "Just As I Am" was a sure sign of grace? Who knows. All I knew was that we were now sitting in a Sunday school class, writing our names on a sheet of paper, and volunteering to bring a casserole to a party on Friday night. The die was cast.

Or so it seemed. In truth, I shouldn't have worried. For in the days that followed, two events took place that changed radically my perception of the church. The first was the party on Friday night, which we went to—casserole in tow and still feeling swept along by the current—and which we surprisingly enjoyed a great deal. In fact, we met some of the finest folks on the face of the earth at that party, including a very special couple who were to become not only grand friends, but a real source of encouragement and help to us in the months that followed.

That fact ushered in the second event, which was every bit as surprising as the first though not nearly as enjoyable. The problem started while I was sitting at the party, chatting with all these wonderful people. "Wow," I said to myself. "These are really bright, fine young Christians. Not a turkey in the crowd. Surely they wouldn't be involved in a church that was practicing membership roulette. Maybe I missed something in the altar call. Maybe I was just being my overcritical self once again, looking for the speck in other people's eyes and forgetting the plank in my own. Maybe the church deserved a second look."

By the time I had finished my introspection, I had not only convinced myself that our initial reaction must have been in error, but I determined to immediately make an appointment to see the pastor and look into the possibility of our becoming members as well.

It wasn't long, then, before I found myself sitting across the desk from Pastor Moe, having a rollicking good discussion about theology and the church and a hundred other things. I even managed to ask about his approach to the altar call, and he assured me that membership was secondary to following Christ and that their first concern at Hillside was to teach the Word of God. Church membership, he said, was important but it was only a means to an end, not the end itself. Their primary objective was to promote the Gospel of Jesus Christ.

I felt greatly reassured by this and told him, if that was the case, then Judy and I were definitely interested in joining their assembly. He was clearly pleased by that and then, almost as if he were shifting gears, he suddenly asked me a question that sounded vaguely familiar: "Stan, are you coming by letter or baptism?"

I was somewhat thrown by this utterly practical question in the midst of a decidedly metaphysical discussion and soon found myself muttering, "Well . . . I'm coming through Christ," or something to that effect, a response which simultaneously amused and annoyed Pastor Moe.

"No, no, no," he broke in laughing. "Of course, you're here because of Christ. But how are you planning to join our church? Are you transferring your membership from another church or do you want to be baptized?"

"Oh," I scratched my head, "well . . . I have already been baptized so I guess I'll be transferring my membership from my home church in California."

"California?" he asked, looking a little worried. "Can you tell me how you were baptized?"

His questions seemed to be growing increasingly practical as well as bizarre, but I knew pastors had to do these things so I decided to play along. "Sure," I said, as I thought about my own baptism. "I was in the first group to be baptized in our church facility. Everyone else in my family was baptized in a reservoir.

CHAPTER 7

But the deacons thought that was a little primitive for a church of our stature so they put an addition on the back of the church with a huge baptismal—"

"Uh, I'm sorry," he broke in once more. "I don't mean to be rude. But I was just wondering whether you were immersed or sprinkled?"

"Oh," I responded, somewhat chastised, "I was immersed."

"And how old were you at the time?" he continued.

"Well, I guess I was about twelve because I know I was in seventh grade. But—excuse me for being rude this time—why do you ask?"

He ignored my question and came back with another. "So you were a Christian at the time you were baptized?"

"Huh?" I reacted naively. "Of course, I was a Christian. Why else would I want to get baptized?" I was beginning to get annoyed. "Not that many Buddhists ask to get baptized in a Christian church, you know. Same for Muslims and atheists. For some reason, that just doesn't seem to appeal to them. In fact—"

"GREAT!" he said, leaning back happily in his chair and ignoring my comment. "So you were baptized by immersion as an adult Christian! That's exactly the way we do it here." He stopped rocking and leaned forward. "So, that means you were baptized in a . . . ?"

I filled in the sentence for him, happily telling him the name and denomination of my home church.

His face must have plunged 20,000 feet. "You mean," he said somewhat flabbergasted, "you're not a member of one of our sister churches?"

"Oh yes," I protested. "It is most definitely a Christian church. In fact, some of the most committed Christians I know come from there."

"No, no, no," he stuttered. "I'm sure it was full of wonderful Christians. But it's not within our tradition, our ilk, our group of churches?"

"Oh no," I laughed. "Definitely not. I come from a church

with a tradition of its own and few there be that find it. In fact, few people even know about it. But it's a wonderful tradition, full of peculiar people who didn't mind being peculiar as long as they were doing what pleased the Lord. It's a heritage that I will cherish all my life, regardless of what church I actually belong to."

"Hummm . . . ," he muttered to himself as I concluded my thoughts about the merits of my own tradition. "In that case I'm afraid you'll have to get baptized in our church to become a member."

"What?" came my quick reply. "But . . . but I've already been baptized. Remember the new church facility? By immersion? As an adult? As a Christian, not a Buddhist? The whole nine yards?"

He let out a deep sigh. "Yes, I know. But you see, to become a member of this church, you must have been baptized in a church within this tradition. That's the rule."

It was a moment of incomprehensibility to me, and so I searched around his office with my eyes, looking for the right words to say. "Look, I can't possibly get baptized again. Not in good conscience. That would be like denying the validity of my first baptism. Besides, I was baptized exactly the same way folks around here are baptized—as I'm sure you were baptized. Would you get baptized again in order to join another church? Would you be willing to trivialize the significance of your baptism like that?"

I could tell from his pained expression that he would not and that he understood my predicament. Suddenly his face brightened, "Look. I've got an idea. There's a church nearby—a sister church of ours—that will accept you just the way you are. They've grown quite tolerant over the years. They'll accept just about anyone these days," he joked. "I'm sure they wouldn't care where you were baptized. Why don't you transfer your membership there and then we can transfer your membership here. We automatically accept anyone who comes from one of our own churches. So then you could come to us by letter. No problem."

We sat there for a moment looking at each other, Pastor Moe

173

appearing like someone who had just solved the mystery of the universe, and I feeling like the universe had never been more inscrutable in all my life. Especially that part of it occupied by Christians. "Let me see if I have this right," I finally said, in slow measured tones. "First you want me to join a church down the road, a church that accepts anything that breathes, I take it, and then you want me to transfer my membership here?"

"Yes!" he said proudly, still grinning from ear to ear.

"So, what you're saying is that if I come from one of your sister churches, I'm in—regardless of my own personal history or background. But if I come from another tradition, I'm out—even if that tradition lines up perfectly with your own church on nearly all matters of faith and practice?"

"That's right!" he said, his smile still as wide and unperturbed as ever.

"Let me be sure I've got this right," I continued. "As far as you're concerned, it's better for me to come from one of your churches than from mine—regardless of how debauched your church may be or how pristine mine may be—simply because it's one of your churches?"

"Well, I wouldn't say 'better.' We're not talking about better here. Shoot, my guess is your home church has a lot more going for it than our sister church down the road. But we're not talking about who has got the best church here. We're talking about membership. And that's a whole different story as far as I'm concerned. A whole different story."

WORSHIPING APART

As I walked out of Pastor Moe's office that day, I felt absolutely drained. I had, of course, politely turned down his offer. But as I shuffled along the church corridor and then out through the portico, I could hardly even keep my head up.

In part, I think that feeling resulted from the emotional roller coaster I had been on over the last few days, first wanting to be a part of Hillside, then thinking they were too membership-oriented for us, finally coming to the conclusion that I could put up with that given everything else Hillside had to offer—and now discovering in one breath that they didn't want me "just as I am," and then in another that they would take me in any condition whatsoever as long as I came from one of their churches. I had known fickle relationships before, but this one took the cake.

But more than the ups and downs, it was the underlying meaning of the thing that really got to me. "Here we have a church that is obviously trying to be faithful to their calling as a church of Christ," I said to myself. "In their statements, in their preaching, in their words, they leave little doubt that they are a people committed to Jesus Christ. His Word is true as far as they are concerned, and they want to build their church on that foundation.

"And yet, when push comes to shove, the building process is really more important than the foundation. In the end, they are far

175

less interested in the authenticity of my faith than the propriety of my credentials. And as important as credentials are, even they are less vital than having another warm body in the pew. The bottom line for this church," I concluded, "isn't the person of Christ. The bottom line isn't even the integrity of the tradition out of which they understand Christ's message. The bottom line is membership, pure and simple. And almost anything seems worth sacrificing to bolster the bottom line."

My head was swimming with disappointment as I stepped off the curb in front of the church and headed across the street toward our apartment. Deep in thought, I'm not much good as a pedestrian, and I soon found myself standing in the middle of the road, with traffic flowing liberally on either side of me and not a chance in a million of ever making it across the tarmac in one piece. Eventually, a kindhearted chap slowed down just enough to enable me to make a break for it, though he gunned his engine the minute I cleared his fender, apparently feeling it necessary to remind me of my stupidity as well his restraint.

"Contemplating suicide?"

The voice came from a parked car, just a few feet from where I had made my escape. I turned to look at the voice, but was blinded by the sun's reflection off the car's front window.

"It's a thought," I said, walking toward the car and wondering with whom in the world I was having this morbid conversation.

"David," came the voice, "David McIntyre. We met at the party last night?" The car door opened, and the voice became embodied in a friendly face and a hearty bearing. "You're Stan, correct?"

"That's right," I said, as I made my way around the car and gave David the right hand of fellowship. "Good memory. How are your classes coming by the way?" I continued, recalling that David was a doctoral student in philosophy at Preppie and wanting to demonstrate that I had remembered at least a portion of our conversation the night before.

"Fine, I think," he grinned, though he followed it up with a quick frown. "It's going to be a tough term, though. My comps are coming up soon and they're always a worry. Thanks for asking." The grin returned. "Hey, why were you trying to get yourself killed on the highway? I know sociology is a dismal discipline," he laughed, "but there are better ways of handling depression than playing on the street."

A quick wit and a ready sense of humor—that's what struck me about David the night of the party. And now, today, it was a balm to my aching spirit, a providential boost if ever there was one.

"Oh, it's nothing really," I lied. "I was just having a chat with Pastor Moe about church membership. I guess I was lost in thought."

David looked at me and winced. "It didn't go well, huh? What happened?"

Another McIntyre trait, I was to learn, was going straight to the heart of the matter. If there was meat on the table, he didn't mess around with appetizers. In fact, he might even bypass the salad and vegetables on any given day. He wanted to get the real stuff, as quickly as possible, and the real stuff today was not graduate school or yesterday's party. The real stuff was across the street, sitting behind a desk in the pastor's study.

"Oh, it went fine, I suppose," I lied again. "Pastor Moe's a fine fellow," I said truthfully, "and I enjoyed our discussion a great deal."

"So, that's why you're trying to kill yourself on the highway? C'mon, Stan. What happened?

"Really, David," I laughed, "it went fine. At least, it went fine until we got to the part about our joining the church. Things sort of fell apart after that. I guess we just didn't see eye-to-eye on the issue of church membership. And that's not really his fault.

Your church just has certain rules about church membership, and I find them a bit perplexing, that's all.''

David looked at me impatiently and, from his expression, I thought he was going to read me the riot act for tip-toeing around the issue. "Why don't you and Judy come over to our house for chili tonight?" he asked instead. "Susan always makes way too much chili anyway. And we've got nothing to do tonight except study and watch our dog back into the heater, neither of which are all that important. What do you say?"

It was more fabrication, of course. I knew the business about studying was a lie, since he had already expressed his concerns about his upcoming exams. But I soon learned that the rest of it was rubbish as well. David never fills up on chili, for one thing; the guy inhales it faster than Susan can put it on his plate. But their dog turned out to be no mean piece of entertainment either. Blessed with a dim mind and poor sense of his own boundaries, the dog was constantly running into things, bouncing off tables and knocking lamps over with his tail.

One of his favorite activities, however, was stretching— placing his forepaws as far as possible in front of him and then extending his hind quarters to their maximum altitude and reach. This was not everyone else's favorite thing, however, as he had a habit of using this position as an opportunity to release more than mere tension. Periodically, he got as much as he gave. And on more than one occasion, he had managed to so misjudge his stretch that he ended up plugging his hind quarters directly into the wall heater. Not being swift of mind, these misjudgments took a while for him to figure out, and so he had a number of significant heater grids emblazoned on his backside. Needless to say, this dog was worth paying attention to. And made our trips to the McIntyres' even more delightful.

"Sounds good," I said, not knowing what was in store for us. "Around sixish?"

"Great," came his quick retort, as he raced across the street toward the church and disappeared through the front doors.

WORSHIPING APART

The dog turned out to be something of a metaphor for our relationship because getting together with the McIntyres became a regular means of stretching and releasing tensions of graduate school pressure. One major difference, however, is that we were never burned by the relationship. Quite the opposite. It was always a time for letting off steam—for laughing at things that only moments before seemed to be of world-shattering importance, for throwing out new ideas that you wouldn't dare mention in any one else's company, for seeking advice on matters great and small, and for just relaxing and sharing space.

And that pattern was set the first evening we got together. For in no time at all, we were laughing and arguing and revealing a lot more of ourselves to one another than we had a right to. But then rights never did have much to do with our friendship. Truth did. And before we were halfway through our second bowl of chili, David had already gotten me to reveal the entirety of my conversation with Pastor Moe, including my own deep disappointment with the outcome.

"I'm just so discouraged about the whole thing," I said, bringing my story to a close. "How can a church put such a high premium on denominational affiliation—so high that they will accept you if you're a member of a sister church, and reject you out of hand if you're not, even if your life is in perfect sync with the teachings and practices of the church? I just don't understand."

"I'm not sure I do either," David said, after I finished my piece, "and I've been a part of the denomination forever. Hearing your story, in fact, makes me wonder how we ever came up with such a policy in the first place. It sure doesn't seem to make sense in your case." He stopped, frowned at his third bowl of chili, and then pushed it away, rocking back in his chair. "Nevertheless, I have to tell you, I do have the feeling—somewhere down in the depths of my being—that on a much broader scale, it might make some sense. I'm not sure I can even articulate it, actually. But that's my hunch."

"Well, maybe," I responded, knowing from the look in

CHAPTER 7

David's eyes that he knew precisely why it made sense but was planning to ease into it gently for the sake of my feelings. "But it seems to me that it's just one more in a long series of obstacles that churches erect that do little more than prevent the church from being the church."

"What do you mean?" David asked, his arched eyebrows suggesting incredulity more than inquiry.

"Well, look, Judy and I have been searching for a permanent church home for over three years, ever since we were married. Now, it is true that for some of that time we weren't all that interested in really plugging into a church. At times, we just wanted to sit in church on Sunday morning and listen. But even if we had wanted more than that, even if we had really wanted to become active members of a church, I doubt we would have been able to manage it."

"Go on," David said as we put away the remaining dishes and walked into the living room. "I'm listening."

"Well, to be honest with you," I raised my voice, "there's just always something immensely wrong or even silly with the churches we have encountered.

"We started out, you see, going to this church that was known for its social involvement. That excited me, being a radical-chic kind of a guy, and I was impressed with their various programs for the poor and their numerous social-action committees. But after we were there on Sunday morning a few times, we wondered why they were doing anything at all. I mean, the pastor didn't have a clue! He'd pull together a bunch of stories, sometimes relate them to a Bible text and sometimes not—it didn't really matter because he rarely seemed to understand the text anyway—and then conclude by telling everyone to go in peace and do whatever was right. But no one had the foggiest notion what was right in that church, nor why they should even be doing it! You wanted to stand up and say, 'Look, folks, Jesus Christ is Lord. *That's* why we're here. *That's* why we're helping the poor.' But had you done that, I'm sure the pastor would have smiled and said, 'That's nice. When is our next committee meeting?' He was absolutely in bonkersville.

"So, anyway, we left that church and began looking around for a real church, where the people took Scripture seriously and had had an encounter with Christ. So we heard about this great church about ten miles from our apartment which was supposedly growing by leaps and bounds, in part because of their great Bible teaching. Well, on our first Sunday we discovered that they were growing all right—and why. The pastor could do nothing but talk about growth. The announcements were about it. The sermon was about it. And when he gave the invitation, it was about church growth as well, as if people were coming forward to swell the numbers on their church rolls. It was absolutely nauseating. True, the pastor knew his Bible. But he was so focused on the issue of church growth, that it seemed to me very little genuine Bible teaching really took place.

"Well, after that we were really discouraged and so . . . ," I stopped to take a breath, "uh, do you really want to hear the rest of this, by the way? It's not the most uplifting story in the world."

"I can take it," David responded with a grin. "Where did you go next?"

"Well, I guess what happened was that we were determined to find a place where the pastor was devoted, first and foremost, to quality biblical exposition. We asked around and discovered that there was a church only a few blocks from us that was known for the quality of its teaching. In fact, the pastor had something of a national reputation. This time when we went, however, we kept our expectations in check. We had heard the line about 'great preaching' before and we were starting to get a bit skeptical.

"As it turned out, this guy was, in fact, a pretty good Bible scholar, and there was no doubt that he really did his homework. He had his message and his delivery down to a science. He also had the benefit of preaching in a church facility that was absolutely gorgeous—you got the feeling that anyone who stepped into that podium would have sounded like a saint. Nevertheless, both Judy

181

and I discovered something after we had gone there for a few months: neither of us could ever remember what the preacher had said, even a few hours after the message. It was all so nice and articulately delivered that it seemed to sail right in one ear and out the other. Everybody sat there, absolutely enthralled by the pastor, seemingly hanging on every word, but as far as we could tell the words were just 'blah, blah, blah.'

"Actually, he sounded so wonderful and the sanctuary was so inspiring, that we probably could have put up with it (for all we knew, we were the problem, not his sermons) except that, about the same time we discovered that we didn't know what the pastor's messages were about, we also discovered that the church leaders had apparently concluded that they were perfect, that they were fully sanctified and no longer sinned. That was new to me— having never managed an hour without sin myself, much less a lifetime—and it completely blew me away. A perfectly delivered sermon, I could take, even if it did sound like blah, blah, blah. But a perfectly sinless human being was beyond my comprehension. That I knew was blah, blah, blah. And so we were soon in search of another church.

"Which leads me to—"

David broke in, "You know there is a tradition of perfection-ism in the Christian church, of becoming perfected in Christ—though it doesn't sound quite like what you ran into. Could that be what they meant?"

"Oh, I'm sure it was," I continued, "and I'm sure I quite misunderstood what they meant by the whole thing. But you have to understand that, by this time, we had seen so much unbeliev-able stuff in our search for a decent church, that we thought anything was possible. We just assumed the worst.

"And that gets us to our last experience, which may have been the worst. Having determined that we were not quite ready for perfection, we went looking for a church that was really real, a church full of real people, with real needs, who did real things (like sin) and where there was some sense of spontaneity and humanity.

And boy did we find it. A small little assembly with less than a hundred people, this church took lack of preparation as a mark of high spirituality! If the pastor had given more than a minute of forethought to his message, it would have surprised me. Him too, I think. His sermons were not exactly the alpha and omega of homiletics; in fact, they were without beginning and without end, and contained no discernible direction in between as well. But they were real. Immensely real.

"The interesting thing about the church is how quickly we discovered that the church's spontaneity was actually quite predictable. For example, a portion of the morning service was always devoted to 'prayer requests.' People would stand up and make their needs known, and then they would spend some time in undirected prayer, with people praying for the various requests 'as they felt led.' Well, at first I really liked this because everyone seemed so vulnerable and genuine. But very shortly it became evident that the same people were always making requests, the same people were always praying for them, and only certain kinds of needs were expressed.

"For example, every morning we always got a progress report on Aunt Minnie in Toullieville who had an infected big toe, much aggravated by a corn. And each Sunday, one or two gentlemen in the front would pray in earnest about Aunt Minnie's corn, encouraging the Lord to give immediate attention to this world-shaking problem. Now I'm sure this was a painful thing for Aunt Minnie, and I'm sure the Lord was happy to hear this request. But she lived two thousand miles away, for heaven's sake, and not a soul in the church even knew who she was. We could have saved considerable time and energy if we had just called a doctor in Toullieville, and told him to amputate Aunt Minnie's corn and send us the bill.

"But you got the suspicion that perhaps solving the problem wasn't the issue for these folks anyway, that they sort of liked these big-toe problems. One thing for sure, they didn't like personal issues. In the whole time we were there, I didn't hear one person get up and say, "I need help. I'm really struggling with jealousy. My neighbor seems to buy anything he wants, and I can't even make ends meet. Please pray that the Lord would help me love my neighbor, not envy him." Not once. All we heard about were physical ailments—from puffy toes to failing organs— and the spiritual needs of people 'out there' who needed God's grace and forgiveness. I sometimes wondered why we didn't reduce our prayers to two: Heal us and our friends, Lord, and convert everybody else. Our bodies, their souls.

"The final straw for us, the final Sunday we were there, they decided to do something a little different. After all the prayer requests were made, they asked us to divide up into small groups of about ten, and then pray amongst ourselves for the various needs. Well, I thought that might be an improvement except that we had the two guys who always prayed for Aunt Minnie's toe, and so we got going on that problem right away. Then someone else prayed about a sailor they had met who needed to know the Lord . . . and stop visiting the downtown area. That was followed by a cancer request, a cousin from Melville facing a bypass surgery, and so on. Finally, everything got quiet, and I realized that I was the only one who hadn't yet prayed. I tried desperately to think of someone who was sick but my mind went blank. I then remembered the conversion prayer and began rummaging through my memory for someone I knew who needed to be saved. It quickly dawned on me that *all* my friends in grad school needed the Lord and I was paralyzed by opportunity.

"And so I didn't say anything. And they kept waiting. And I finally realized that this was one of the dumbest situations I had ever been in in my life. Here we were in a church that prided itself on its spontaneity and sincerity, and what was everyone doing? Sitting around waiting for me to take my turn at prayer, waiting for me to enter into one of the strictest liturgies I had ever encountered, a liturgy confined to our bodies and their souls. It was too much. Right then and there, I resolved two things. One, to never again mistake spontaneity for spirituality. And two, that I wasn't about to pray, even if everyone's Sunday dinner was ruined in the process.

"But more than that was resolved, I'm afraid. Because once we finally escaped from that church, we pretty much stopped going to church unless we went to one of our parents' churches. But neither of us has been happy about that outcome. And so we were looking forward to making a fresh start of things here, to finding a new church, to putting all our past failures behind us. And then what happens? Pastor Moe and the fickle fellowship of Hillside Church, that's what happens—one more in a long string of churches doing everything it can to keep the Gaedes from enjoying the fellowship of the body of Christ.

"And you know what, David?" I said, after I had a chance to collect my thoughts and take a reading on David's reaction. "It just doesn't seem right. Or fair. In fact, if truth be known, I suppose I'm sort of angry with God for leading us into this kind of thing one more time. But I'm not all that happy with your church either, David. In fact, if you want to know the truth, I think your church's rule on membership is downright smelly. I think it kind of stinks."

WORSHIPING THE LORD

"Look Stan," David said, in tones much less passionate than mine and far more reflective, "I think it 'rots' as well. I think you ought to be able to join our church as you are, without having to jump through a bunch of organizational hoops. And if it would make any difference, I'd go over to Pastor Moe's office tomorrow and tell him so—"

"No, David," I broke in. "I mean, it really 'rots' in here. Something smells rotten!"

"Oh, it's the dog," said Susan, as she and Judy strolled in the room, having completed their evening constitutional around the block. "The dog is not discreet. Nor smart. Nor much good, actually. In fact, we're not quite sure why we have this dog. But we do. And what you're smelling is one of the benefits. It'll pass . . . ready for dessert?" And before anyone could answer, Susan was off to the kitchen whomping up some whipped cream and creating strawberry shortcake.

"My wife does not mince words," David put in, almost by way of apology.

"She's great!" I responded. "I love her already."

"Me too," was David's quick reply, his eyes dancing like a five-year-old at a chocolate factory. "But it won't make any difference."

"Huh?" I questioned, trying to figure out his point.

"Going to Pastor Moe's office?" David continued. "It won't make any difference," he repeated, as I nodded my head in agreement, finally realizing that he was back in our former conversation. "And there's a good reason. Pastor Moe doesn't make the rules around here any more than I do. The policies of our church are determined by the congregation, and the congregation is operating out of a whole tradition of decision making. So one doesn't shift gears on a policy like this, at least not very quickly."

David stopped for a second and gave me a quizzical look, almost as if he were trying to figure out whether he should continue. "And—at the risk of incurring your wrath—I have to tell you, I'm glad about that. Because I don't believe churches should flip-flop too easily on basic policy. And because, on the whole, I believe church traditions are valuable things.

"Take your situation, for example," David continued. "You're upset because, on the one hand, we are very open about taking in new members from other sister churches, but very strict about requiring a confession of faith and baptism from people who are coming in from the outside. And in your case, that doesn't sound fair. Nor is it, in my opinion.

"But if we step back for a second, it makes all kinds of sense as a general policy. We live in a world, and a society, containing an awful lot of strange churches, many of which call themselves Christian. Your own journey makes that clear. You cannot be confident that, just because people say they follow Christ, that they have gotten anything like true Christian teaching in the process, right? And so, long ago our churches decided that to make sure that people knew the score beforehand, we would require a number of things of them, including baptism (which we take rather seriously). They did not mean by this to deny the validity of anyone's past experience. They only wanted to make sure that new members understood clearly what we believed before they entered into our fellowship.

"Now, of course, that raises the question, If we're so concerned about correct doctrine, then why do we let almost anyone in our church if they happen to be coming from one of our sister churches?"

I nodded my head in agreement.

"That's a good question," he continued, "not only because it seems puzzling but because it says a lot about where we've come in the last few years. The fact is, when this policy was instituted, you could pretty much count on the fact that all churches within our denomination were in agreement on the basics. So drawing the line where we did made some sense at the time. But over the years, churches have increasingly gone their own way, chasing various new ideas that have come down the pike—or reacting against them, which has been just as bad sometimes—and breaking down the old consensus.

"So now we have people coming to our church, like you, who are from another tradition, but are closer to our own beliefs, than some of the folks in our sister churches. So what do we do? If I read you correctly, Stan, you would have us throw out the policy altogether and simply accept anyone who was a genuine Christian, regardless of their background. Is that right?"

"You got it, David," I chimed in quickly. "That's what Jesus does. And if it's good enough for Jesus, it ought to be good enough for those who claim to be his followers."

"I'm not so sure," David came back at me in a surprising move, surprising because I thought he was going to disagree with Jesus. "Jesus certainly accepts all those who genuinely seek him—or better yet, all who respond to his seeking, since he's the one who pursues us, not vice versa. But Jesus has a big advantage over us: He knows the heart. He knows whose faith is genuine, we do not. We only have pieces of evidence—the fruit of the Spirit, in particular—and over time we can put this evidence together and make some pretty good guesses.

"But when someone comes to your church and says, 'Let me in,' at that point the evidence is paltry. It's especially paltry if all you can do is believe their words, since words are very malleable things, especially in the modern world. People mouth the right words because they've grown up with them, absorbed them by osmosis. Others say the wrong words, not because their faith isn't genuine but because their culture is different. So it is very hard to decide the whole matter on a few words. And thus, we require more than words. We require the act of baptism of everyone, an act which requires one to go through the Gospel story with one's body, to feel it, to testify to it, and hopefully to understand what you're getting yourself into."

"But that doesn't assure anything!" I broke in. "People can lie with their bodies as well as their words."

"Of course they can. But the point isn't to make absolutely sure that they're Christians. That's in God's hands. We don't hold the keys to the kingdom. The point is to make sure we've done our part to communicate the Gospel, to let them know what they're in for ahead of time."

"Okay, I see your point here," I admitted, "but it still seems strange to automatically let someone in if they're from a sister church, especially given the direction some of these churches have gone. Doesn't that contradict the purpose of your church's tradition?"

"Yes it does," David responded quickly. "No doubt about it. Something's got to change soon or we're in trouble. The question is, Should Hillside change its tradition and simply go off on its own path in order to solve the problem? Or should Hillside stay within the larger denomination and try to get its sister churches to live up to the tradition of which they are a part? In other words, should we chuck our tradition out the window to get a few more members like you? Or should we risk losing people like you in order to bring about reform in the larger church body?"

"And you think the latter?" I asked, knowing from David's tone that I already had my answer.

"Well," he said, again apologetically, "I'm afraid I do. Not that you're not important. I'd love to have you in our church! But you have other options. You can, if necessary, go somewhere else.

CHAPTER 7

We, on the other hand, are dealing with the future of an entire tradition, a future that I think is very much in doubt right now."

"But why, in heaven's name," I blurted out, "is the tradition so bloomin' important to you? Why hang on to it if it's not working?"

David leaned forward and grimaced, as if he were about to say something that he knew I wouldn't understand, or wouldn't like, but felt he had to say anyway. "Because it *is* important, Stan. The tradition *is* valuable.

"Look," he continued. "You think of the tradition as blind ritual. But it isn't, or shouldn't be. Tradition is simply another word for people—a people trying to be faithful to a heritage, to a calling. But this is not just any old heritage. This is an attempt of a people to be faithful to Jesus Christ. Besides, the problem isn't that the tradition isn't working; the problem is that we're not living up to the standards of the tradition. We're not putting the tradition into practice.

"You see, Stan, you think that when things don't work out perfectly in the church, the thing to do is change the rules, to change the tradition. But I think it is precisely that tendency that has gotten us into trouble in the first place. Why is it that you can go out there," he said, pointing to the world beyond his house, "and find four million brands of churches, some of them just strange, many downright heretical? Because at some point things weren't working out right, from someone's point of view. And so that person said, 'I've got a better idea. Let's change the rules. Let's get rid of the tradition and start something new.' What seems far preferable to me—but what seems difficult to do in today's atmosphere—is to ask: How can we make the tradition come alive again? How can we breathe new life into it, so that it accomplishes its intended purpose?

"But, alas, very few seem interested in that alternative these days," he said, leaning back in his chair once again. "In fact," he said, looking at me disbelievingly, "it probably doesn't even make

190

any sense to you when I explain it—especially not to you, since you've been the victim of my beloved tradition."

I looked down at the floor, noticing that the dog was about the stretch in my direction. "I guess," I answered, at the same time leaping off the couch and moving to the other side of the room, "with my heart I find it hard to understand . . . but, you know, with my mind I kind of do. In fact, sociologically it makes quite a bit of sense. One of the problems with our world is—"

"There are too many philosophers and sociologists!" Susan chimed in, as she and Judy came back into the room, this time with Everest-size shortcakes in their hands.

"Actually, Stan," Susan continued, not giving us a minute to defend ourselves and locating herself in the seat I had just vacated, "I was talking with Judy about your church experiences, and I do think I know what your problem is: You guys have become church connoisseurs! You've seen so many churches, you've compared them so diligently, that it's easy for you to spot the weaknesses of any particular church and hard for you to be satisfied with the church you're at. It's just like shopping. If you get really good at it, you're never satisfied. You always want something a little better.

"What you need to do," she continued, "is find a good church and stick with it. Stop asking what's wrong with the church and start asking what are the needs there and how can you help. After all, a church isn't a place where you go to get something—like filling up with a tank of gas. A church is a place where you go to give: to give praise to God, to give encouragement to other Christians, to serve the needy, to teach, to pray, and so on. As long as you and Judy go to church just to hear a sermon or get some kind of a blessing, you're going to be disappointed. That's not the point of church, in my humble opinion."

Under some circumstances, if someone had spoken that directly to me, I would have taken offense. When Susan said it, however, I just smiled, and listened, and waited in eager anticipation for her encounter with the full effects of her pet.

CHAPTER 7

"Susan, I doubt you have a humble opinion in your entire being!" I responded. "And I doubt you'll want to sit there for long, either."

And it was all true. Susan moved quickly for one thing. But Susan told the truth, as well. And in one quick slice, she had cut through all my rhetoric about disappointing churches and disappointing Christians and gotten to the heart of the matter. And the heart of the matter was me. Me, with my grand ideals about the perfect church. Me, with the assumption that the church was there to live up to my standards, not the other way around. I didn't accept that verdict right away, of course. The disappointments were too great for me to conclude that the pain was self-inflicted. But it came with time. And with the gracious yet prickly assistance of the Holy Spirit.

In saying that, of course, I do not wish to whitewash the sins of the church, which are legion. What we encountered on our journey in those days was not the church at its best. It was church in search of numbers, not ministry. Church captured by narrow self-interest, not the interests of its Lord. Church aping the ways of the world, not penetrating it with salt and light and the transforming power of Jesus Christ. It was, in other words, a church beset with all the problems of the world that it was there to serve.

And yet, if our analysis stops there, then we have done little more than provide an excuse for inaction—a reason to sit on our hands and do nothing, to become a part of the problem and not the solution. And more importantly, our analysis would be wrong. Because, you see, David and Susan were clearly on the mark: church for us had become an individual matter, designed for our convenience and enjoyment. We had become, as Susan said, connoisseurs. Church shoppers. Trying on various brands and looking for the best fit. And I was, as David gently reminded me, more interested in my own individual happiness than in the future of that tradition, the future of their church.

WORSHIPING THE LORD

Church is a problem. There's no doubt about that. But the biggest problem with it, I have come to believe, is that it is full of people like me—who want the church to be an inspiring bit of weekend entertainment—and increasingly depleted of people like David and Susan, for whom the church is the body of Christ. Full of imperfections and defects because it is full of people. But full of opportunities as well. Opportunities to worship. Opportunities to serve. Opportunities to use the gifts that God has undeservedly showered upon his people, not so that we might look good on Sunday morning, but so that the Sovereign God of the universe might look good through us, every hour of every day. And so that the world might know—by looking at us, his church—that Jesus Christ is Lord. And we are not.

CHAPTER 8
DISCOVERING SUCCESS

ANXIETY

I have a friend who's short. On its own, that isn't noteworthy. No more significant than the fact that John is tall, Mary has a small nose, and Stan is as skinny as a rail. But we live in a world enamored by averages. And because Eric is shorter than average, it is something with which he must contend.

Contending with a physical fact such as this seems to bring out the worst in some of us. We become angry at God for making us so skinny or angry at others for making judgments about us based on how we look. Sometimes, however, contending with our differences brings out the best in us—and that has certainly been the case with my friend. Never once have I heard him complain about his height, either to God or to others. In fact, he seems to enjoy it.

For instance, one weekend Eric went to church with a friend. His friend's church was one of those places that insists on welcoming everyone from the pulpit, and so Eric and all other visitors were asked to stand up and be recognized. The church was loaded with visitors that morning, so it took some time for the pastor to get around to everyone, asking them their name, where they were from, and so on. Finally, the pastor managed to greet every visitor in the church except Eric, who stood patiently in the back of the church, waiting his turn.

Before Eric could introduce himself, however, the pastor

moved on to the next part of the service, ignoring Eric altogether. Under such circumstances, most of us would have sat down and fumed—or in my case, thanked the Lord for his manifold blessings. But Eric did none of those things. Instead, he waved his hand until he caught the attention of the pastor. Eventually, the pastor looked up from his bulletin and noticed Eric. Realizing his mistake, the pastor quickly launched into an apology.

"I'm so sorry, young man," intoned the pastor. "I completely missed you sitting back there. Please, why don't you stand up and introduce yourself."

Eric didn't miss a beat. "I am standing!" he shot back with a laugh and a grin the size of Texas.

The pastor was now really embarrassed, and with innumerable apologies, he again asked Eric his name.

"Zacchaeus!" was Eric's quick response, after which the entire congregation doubled over with laughter.

I love Eric, and people like him. People who are able to laugh at themselves. People who are secure enough not to take offense when offense was not intended. People who are wise enough to know that the world's values are not worth taking all that seriously in the first place. People who, out of their security and wisdom, are able to turn the world on its head, laughing at what the world would call a tragedy and leaving the rest of us wondering how they are able to do it.

That isn't the way it is with most of us, is it? Our insecurities are so near the surface that the moment anyone even comes near them we start to bellow.

At least, I do. As a professor and an author, I am required to execute my responsibilities in public. That is, when I teach I am expecting to be standing in front of a classroom full of students, and when I write I am hoping that someone out there will one day want to read the words I am putting down on paper. Those hopes and expectations are not always fulfilled. Students sometimes prefer the beach to my class. And publishers sometimes choose to spare the world my prose. But if students and publishers boycotted my efforts for long, I would eventually have to move into another line of work. Because the purpose of writing and teaching is communication, and communication is a two-way street.

So, as I say, I have a very public occupation. That means that my wares are regularly on display, out there and available for public inspection. I don't always mind, of course. I especially don't mind when people say things I want to hear. The other day, for example, a student walked into my office and proclaimed that I was a great artist. Having absolutely no artistic talent whatsoever—I can't even write legibly on the blackboard—I asked her what she meant. She went on to say that I wove my lectures together like musical compositions, that my classes were works of art and she never got tired of them.

Well, needless to say, that student received an "A." I even offered to pay her tuition next term—anything to keep the accolades coming. But my good mood was short-lived, because the student that followed her into my office was convinced that I constructed my exams with the expressed purpose of undermining his grade-point average and his alone. For some reason (I try to block these things out), my test questions were not suited to his learning style. That was my fault, apparently, because he was pulling good grades from every prof on campus except me. I offered to use pictures instead of words on my next exam, but he was not amused. Nor would he leave. In fact, he was not satisfied until he had picked apart each and every question on the exam, telling me precisely why the thing was so poorly worded and how it could have been constructed differently. By the time he left, I was convinced that I could neither teach nor write.

And it bugged the tar out of me. "Who is he?" I said to myself. "Doesn't he know I'm a great artist? Hasn't he heard that I weave together breathtaking compositions in the classroom?" And before I knew it, I was in a deep funk, doubting my calling and treating everyone in the hall as if they were out to get me. ("Good morning, Dr. Gaede," a student innocently says. "No it isn't," says I.) Now you have to wonder how it is that an adult human being can go from euphoria to a life crisis in a matter of minutes after talking with two very different people, both of whose comments were no doubt motivated more by their own needs than by my performance. Why didn't I just say thanks for the accolade as well as the criticism, count the first as a pat on the back and the second as a useful piece of advice?

Because I'm deeply insecure, that's why. And having watched three children grow up now, I can tell you why: I was once a child, living in the jungle of child-dom. I mean, do you have any idea what children do to one another?

Kirsten came home yesterday with a salamander in her hand. She is seven, so these are the days of frogs, snails, snakes, and salamanders. Apparently she found the little fellow in the stream that runs behind our neighbors' house. Actually, her neighborhood friend was the one who really found the guy, but in an attempt to get it to perform some salamanderish feat, he accidentally stunned him instead—so much so that they thought it was going to die. Since Kirsten is preparing for a career in the health sciences, she immediately began applying mouth-to-mouth resuscitation ("I gave it PPR, Dad . . ."), blowing air into its mouth and pushing its stomach back in with her little finger when it seemed sufficiently bloated. If this had been our first child, I would have fainted, after which the child would have had her stomach pumped at the local hospital. This is our third, however, so I just patted her on the head, grabbed the Alka Seltzer and kept listening. Anyway, the long and short of it is that she saved the salamander's life, and as a reward, her friend allowed her to take care of it for a few days.

As you can imagine, the salamander became something of an icon for Kirsten, and her fingers soon took the form of a tin can, so often and so firmly did they clutch that salamander's home. In fact, she looked a bit like a beggar, carrying that tin can around with her all over the place, except that instead of crying, "Alms,

CHAPTER 8

alms," she said, "Look, look," and repeated the story of the salamander's salvation and her successful execution of "PPR." Needless to say, when she awoke the next morning, she wanted to take it to school with her and present the salamander as her offering at show-and-tell.

Now, I can't fathom how anyone can teach elementary school. I can't even imagine teaching high school, myself, having my hands full with college students who pay fabulous sums to listen to me and supposedly want to be there. But first grade is just beyond comprehension. I'm especially amazed that someone trying to handle thirty first graders would have a portion of the day dedicated to show-and-tell. That's like a chicken farmer telling a fox that it can have free run of the chicken house for thirty minutes every morning. I mean, showing and telling is what kids live for and what parents all over the world do their best to avoid! But first-grade teachers not only allow it, they have institutionalized the process, insuring themselves of thirty minutes of the most incoherent babbling known to man and no small number of shocks.

Like a salamander from Kirsten—which her father reluctantly told her she could take to school, *if* she left it in the box, and *IF* it was okay with her teacher, and after repeated assurances of total sanctification on her part and the sovereignty of God on his own (parents tend be Arminians when talking to their children and Calvinists when talking to themselves). Well, the teacher turned out to be an Arminian that day as well, which meant that she wasn't going to take any chances with a salamander and thirty children. The minute she saw Old Sal, therefore, she politely told Kirsten that the classroom was not the place for it, and that after showing it to the other children, she should release it someplace out on the playground.

This, of course, was a very wise thing for a first-grade teacher to do, and I'm sure it came from years of experience with various sorts of slimy creatures slithering down the hall with ten thousand children slithering after it. Nevertheless, Kirsten was

200

dumbfounded. In the first place, she thought the classroom was the perfect place for a salamander. After all, that's where "show-and-tell" was considered legitimate entertainment. But secondly, she was convinced that there was only one proper home for Sal, and that was near the river from which he had originally been retrieved (she's into environmental science as well). What was inconceivable to her was the idea that he would be let out on the playground, where there was no river whatsoever, but where there were hordes of children who couldn't even keep from stepping on their own feet, much less a little salamander desperately trying to find his way home.

By the time Kirsten walked out onto the playground to let the little guy loose, therefore, she felt she was at the bottom of a giant pit of despair. She was wrong, however. The bottom was yet to come. You will remember that the salamander did not belong to her—that she had it on loan from her friend who had graciously allowed her to play with it for a day or so after her resuscitation feat. Well, naturally, when he found out that Kirsten had let Sal go, he was beside himself with righteous indignation, informing her—in no uncertain terms—that their days of friendship and camaraderie had permanently come to an end (translation: "I won't play with you today . . . at least not until I've had my snack").

To make matters worse, when she got on the bus to come home that afternoon, someone wrote a dirty word on the back window and blamed Kirsten. That seemed like a good idea to all the other kids sitting near the window, so they all chimed in and blamed her as well, including a few that Kirsten thought were her best friends. Fortunately, the bus driver didn't believe them and she was at least spared the indignity of an adult reprimand. But by the time she walked into the house, she not only knew that she was without Sal, she was pretty sure she was without much of a reason for living as well.

SECURITY

All of this got me thinking about insecurity, right? Well, it probably would have if something else hadn't happened, something that resulted in my pondering—not insecurity—but of all things prayer.

When Kirsten woke up the next morning, she had nearly recovered from the salamander incident. She was still worried about Sal, of course, out there on the grass flats of the playground desperately trying to find his way home in the midst of hundreds of legs. But I told her that salamanders had a knack for locating a good marsh (which seemed like a reasonable thing to say at the time), and she took comfort in the story of Lassie ("Sal Come Home"). Besides, she had already accomplished a modest reconciliation with her friend, and while they weren't exactly bosom buddies yet, they were at least playing in the vicinity of one another.

One thing still worried her, though, and that was the bus. The dirty-word incident had left her paralyzed with fear, no doubt because as a first grader she was one of the youngest on the bus and fully intimidated by the big kids who occupied the back. I offered her great words of wisdom—"Don't sit in the back of the bus"—and she replied with some of her own—"The front is already full when I get on." I responded with more brilliant ideas—"Get out to the bus stop early so you can be first in line"—

202

all of which were countered decisively—"Most of the kids are already *on* the bus before it gets to us, Daddy." I've discovered that no matter how much older or more brilliant parents are than their children, they cannot win such contests. And so on about the twenty-fifth decisively defeated suggestion, I said, "Do what you want. You're on your own."

"No, I'm not!" she said enthusiastically, no doubt pleased that once again I had been bested. "Jesus is in my heart."

That one stopped me in my tracks. I wanted desperately to play the same game she had so successfully played against me, countering her only positive statement with a negative reply of my own. But this was not the kind of comment I could counter. Nor wanted to. So I just sat there, looking stupid and happy and defeated all at the same time, and said nothing whatsoever.

". . . So," Kirsten continued reflectively, and then suddenly pointed to the heavens, ". . . I could pray! That's what I'll do. I'll ask the Lord to protect me and give me a seat near the front of the bus." And before I could arm her with all the appropriate qualifications—"That's good, Kirsten, but don't expect the Lord to do your work for you; and remember, he doesn't always give us precisely what we want; sometimes our wants don't correspond to his will and sometimes . . . blah, blah, blah . . ."—she slipped on her coat and backpack, gave me a kiss good-bye, and boldly marched out the door. It was as if she had been suddenly transformed from a cowering little urchin into a tower of strength and was now fully prepared to take on the entire world.

Of course, I had not been so transformed. As she left the house and I watched her promenade to the bus stop, I couldn't help but worry about her future. I've learned over the years that the kids on the back of the bus do not change their spots overnight. I know that in part because I have been their victim. I know it as well because I joined the club during my more mature years. And vacant seats in the front of the bus don't just suddenly appear either. Kids that sit there tend to be habitualists in the extreme, inclined neither toward experimentation nor absenteeism. In fact, I remember being rather surprised to see them stand, they seemed so glued to their seats. The point is, I was not hopeful and in fact a bit worried.

Now if you know anything about the way the Lord works in our family, you already know the end of this story. Because whenever there's a contest between my worries and someone else's faith, the Lord always sides with the faithful. Always. Consequently, when Kirsten came home from school that afternoon, I should have just assumed that the Lord had taken care of everything. In fact, I probably should have assumed that he had emptied the entire front section of the bus for her—or gotten her a private limo for that matter. But I am a slow learner. And an eager worrier. And so no such assumption made its way anywhere near my brain, and the minute she walked in the door, I expected to hear the worst.

"Well, Hon, how'd it go today?" I asked cautiously.

"Great!" she said enthusiastically. "I got the book I was looking for at the library. Laura was back in school today. We learned about reptiles and lizards and good stuff like that. And my teacher said—"

"Uh, good," I said, interrupting her stream of consciousness. "But I was wondering about the bus. How did the bus ride go today?"

She looked at me kind of bewildered, and then her eyes brightened up. "Oh, yah," she said, as if she were recalling an event that occurred during the last Ice Age. "Great! Everything went great! I got a seat right by the bus driver this morning, just like I prayed for. But I don't think I needed it because everyone seemed to be in a good mood today. Great day. What's for snack, Dad? Did you eat *all* the cookies again, Dad? You promised to save some for me! And what happened to the chocolate milk, Dad? DAD . . . ?"

There is no need to go on with this story. You know who ate the cookies as well as the chocolate milk. The same guy who spent the entire day worrying about his daughter rather than getting his

SECURITY

work done or keeping his hands out of the cookie jar. The anxious one. The one with four million qualifications for every prayer. The one who is very good at figuring out why a problem can't possibly be solved and pretty bad at leaving his anxiety in the hands of the Lord.

Why is that anyway? It isn't because I'm afraid to pray or doubt God's willingness to hear and respond. In fact, I pray regularly. And not because I feel obligated, but because I want to. I relish my early morning hour with the Lord. And I have seen so many prayers answered over the years that I don't doubt for a second either the power of prayer or the faithfulness of God to those who seek him. No. The problem is not the effectiveness of prayer but the way I so often find myself thinking about it.

Take the results of prayer, for example. I'm compelled to testify that I see a relationship between my prayer life and my well-being. Prayer makes a difference. When I bring things to the Lord in prayer, laying them at his feet honestly, I almost always see results. Not the results I originally assumed would be forthcoming, necessarily, and certainly not always the empty seat in the front of the bus for Kirsten. But results, nevertheless, clearly indicating that God is at work in my life and that the work he is accomplishing—often in spite of me—is good.

But that's a bit of a problem for me because, when I step back and take a look at that equation, it seems to be something of a theology of works. That is, it sounds as if I have to do something to get God to respond, that my well-being is, in the end, dependent more upon what I do than upon what God does. More than that, I don't think it sheds a very positive light on the Lord either. After all, is he some reluctant suitor in the sky, who won't love you unless you love him first? Is he sitting up there, waiting for you to pray in order to respond? Worse yet, is he causing distress in my life just to get me to pray, threatening me with all kinds of calamities if I don't buckle under and ask him for his help?

I can really relate to that last comment these days, because in the last few weeks I have been the victim of one expensive tragedy

205

after another. First, the heating system in the house expired; that turned out to be a three thousand dollar job at least, four thousand if we do it right. Then one of the children God gave me crashed into the back of a jeep with our car; that would have been fine if jeeps weren't equipped with spare tires hanging off their backsides, just high enough to miss your front bumper and just low enough to crease your hood. Then my fancy new printer decided to produce lines instead of prose. As the repairman handed me a bill for five hundred dollars, he comforted me with the thought that these are usually very reliable machines and he'd never seen even an old one with such a problem before. I felt special.

And of course, you want to scream, especially if you've got a child in college and you're up to your eyeballs in debt. Is God trying to tell me something, I wondered? Am I not praying enough? Is he using all of these frightfully difficult circumstances to bring me to my knees? Is God really as vindictive as that? Not a few Christians I have listened to over the years seem to give an affirmative response to that question, by the way. They assume that God causes evil in their lives to prod them to do something, or be something, or learn something, and they glowingly give thanks to the Lord afterward for his marvelous work.

I don't doubt for a second that God is at work in the lives of such people, but I must tell you I have difficulty with their reasoning. God is the author of life, the giver of every good and precious gift. He abhors evil, can't stand the sight of it. What he does is unswervingly deemed good in the Bible. In fact, the very meaning of "goodness" for the Christian is synonymous with the nature of God. That is why he is called Holy. And therefore I find the language of "God causing evil" to be both theologically repugnant and biblically unsound. Quite wrong, in other words.

And yet, isn't that what we come to if we take this matter of prayer seriously? If good things happen to me when I pray and bad things happen when I do not, then am I not being rewarded for praying and punished for failing to pray? And then can't we say that God is using evil to bring me to my knees? And am I not, in turn, using prayer to garner his favor and mollify his wrath? In other words, doesn't the effectiveness of prayer leave us precisely in the conundrum of believing God causes evil on the one hand, and believing that I can manipulate God into doing what I want on the other?

The answer, I think, can be found on the bus that hauls Kirsten back and forth to school every day. For there we discover the missing ingredient in all these questions about prayer as well as my own anxiety. It takes the form of human beings, children in this case, who do wrong and then blame it on others. Who write dirty words on the back window—thinking it will improve their status—and then blame the kid in the next seat. Who eat fruit from the tree of good and evil, in other words, thinking it will make them like God, and then blame it on the person nearby. It is sin, in the language of the ages, and from all accounts it is not an insignificant force in our world. Its Promoter prowls around like a hungry lion, we are told, seeking those whom he might devour. He is strong and his sway can be seen everywhere, not only on the bus, but in the boardroom, in the statehouse, in the classroom, and in the home. He is there, not by accident but by invitation, and wherever his influence reaches, there go hate and envy, oppression and injustice, lust and pride, pain upon pain, evil upon evil.

For that reason, the bus is not an easy place to be. It is a playground for the Evil One, a battleground for conflict between good and evil, assuming good is brave enough to make a showing. Nevertheless, it is a bus we must ride if we are human beings and a conflict we must enter if we are Christians. We cannot avoid it by staying home from school every day, nor can we pretend that the battle isn't being waged. Our only options are to join the battle or join the Enemy. And we make our choices every day.

It is not a metaphor we much appreciate these days, is it? In fact, it's a picture we humans have consistently tried to avoid over the years. By blaming others, in the first instance. But by denying its accuracy, more recently. And so we say that the children on the bus have a poor self-image, and need to think more positively

207

about themselves (which they might). Or the windows were overly grimy, we say, inviting eager fingers to place designs in their midst; they need to be maintained better or redesigned (which they might). And thus we spend our time boosting egos and replacing windows, all of which may be helpful and necessary things to do, but none of which will make a dime's worth of difference in the overall outcome of the battle. Or in the substance of our condition.

But in the midst of the battle, according to that same irritating old story, we have a Resource. More than a resource, he is the Sovereign God of history, the Creator of heaven and earth, the one who fashioned us in his image in the first place, giving us the option of honoring him rather than the necessity, and allowing the battle to exist—or enduring it, we might better say—as a result. He could have done it differently. He could have created automatons that would have honored him without reflection. But he didn't. He created willful beings instead, who could choose to love him. Or try to depose him and play at being gods themselves. We have chosen the latter option, all of us, and thus the battle rages. It rages because we are not God. It rages because God will not allow us to live comfortably with our pretensions. It rages because he keeps sending us reminders of our delusions—people on the bus who get hurt by our behavior, people in the world who starve because of our greed, people in the office who are diminished by our gain—people who remind us that things are not the way they should be.

But he gives us more than reminders, for he has also joined the battle. Giving us aid when we decide to fight for the right. Weaving his goodness into the very fabric of his creation, so that evil always ends up consuming itself, and God's irrepressible splendor and grace and beauty always shine through. And most amazingly of all, taking our form, sharing our pain, bearing our sins, dying the death we deserve, providing for our salvation, so that evil could be conquered—is being conquered—and so that the final victory over sin is assured. Why? Because he's God. So that those who love him will be able to do so forever.

And so we pray, we Christians. We pray. Not to prevent God from inflicting evil upon us, which makes no sense. But to prevent evil from having its way in our lives. Without prayer, we go to the battle poorly equipped. We try to fight it without the necessary armor. And should we do so, and should we receive wounds as a result, it will not do for us to blame our condition on the One who graciously offers us his protection. He did not set the battle in motion, after all. And he has rather gone out of his way—indeed, paid a fairly stiff price—to enable us to wage the battle as it is.

No. We pray because we need help. We pray because we cannot win the battle on our own. We pray because we cannot lose the battle if the Lord is on our side—or more precisely, when we join forces with him. And we give thanks, even when the battle goes poorly, because we know without a shadow of a doubt the final outcome, and we can't wait to join the victory party. We pray, in other words, because it would be pretty dumb to do otherwise.

The problem we face is neither a God who threatens us with evil if we don't pray, nor a poor self-image that needs a boost. The problem is sin. And the solution we have at hand is nothing less than the One who has overcome the sins of the world. With such a Champion in the midst of the battle, a warrior can run and not be weary. A father can pray and not be anxious. A child can march to the bus stop and not be afraid. And a shorter-than-average friend can say, "My name is Zacchaeus," and enjoy the laughter.

SUCCESS

"Can" is the operative word in the last sentence, and it is sometimes quite a long trip between "can" and "will."

I learned that during my last year at Preppie University. Despite all our ups and downs, our time at Preppie had been good. We made some wonderful friends there, certainly. Judy's year as a kindergarten teacher, followed by a year-and-a-half as a full-time mother and husband-healer, had gone well. Our lean budget, especially after Heather was born, seemed to be regularly replenished with unexpected scholarships, unexpected jobs and unexpected gifts. What seemed like a plunge into bankruptcy at the beginning turned out to be a modest step into short-term debt, and the government even volunteered to forgive half of the debt when I decided to venture into higher education.

Even graduate school—that institution that lured us halfway across the country in the first place and which has a well deserved reputation for sado-masochistic behavior—was not only tolerable but really quite enjoyable. I have mentioned elsewhere that portions of my academic career were not sterling, especially those years that fell between kindergarten and college. That's a considerable amount of time by anyone's accounting, and one suspects that some important things are supposed to be learned then. At the least, one is not supposed to wake up in graduate school and suddenly begin functioning as a scholar, much less enjoy it. But that is essentially what happened to me. And I did enjoy it. Immensely.

Success in scholarship is not unlike success anywhere else. It is accompanied by both internal and external rewards. The internal rewards are those inherent in the scholarly task itself, such as the exhilaration of understanding a concept for the first time or pulling together a research project or advancing a line of thought in some way. These are the kinds of rewards that you don't experience until you actually become absorbed in your craft. Just as you must learn the skills of a mechanic before you can know the satisfaction of deciphering the problem in a quirky engine, so you must become a student before you can know the pleasure of mastering *Macbeth* or cracking Durkheim. But precisely because internal rewards require such immersion, they are more enjoyable when attained and more worthy in the long run.

And no doubt increasingly rare. For it is not the internal rewards that consume most of our attention in the modern world. That is reserved for external rewards: the paycheck at the end of the week, the grades at the end of the term, the name in the newspaper, the trophy on the edge of the desk, the reputation in the eyes of the world. These are the things that often lure us into a position in the first place. And increasingly these are the things that keep us there, or keep us looking for new positions, or keep us dissatisfied with the position we're in. Certainly, they are the things that are considered glamorous in our culture. And it would be an odd thing indeed if most of us did not succumb to their seductions.

My journey as a student, however, was somewhat unusual in that for a considerable length of time I pursued neither internal nor external rewards. That is, I continued along in school, neither for enjoyment nor for career advancement. I just continued. I now count that to be a minor miracle, but in retrospect it seems immensely odd. In fact, it is so strange that it may be quite wrong. That is, it may be that there were enough flashes of enjoyment along the way (and I do recall a few) and enough career aspirations

211

to keep me going. That would seem to make sense, though I can't verify it in retrospect. What I do remember quite clearly is suddenly waking up to the sheer pleasure of learning sometime during my later years in college but without the vaguest idea of how I might package that pleasure into a career.

The important thing about this confusion over external rewards is that it enabled me to escape the usual reasons people go on to graduate school and to become a student instead. In other words, through no merit of my own, I suddenly found myself pursuing a scholarly path for almost entirely internal reasons. And thus, when I started grad school at Blah University, I had no idea what I would do with my education nor why (externally speaking now) I was doing it. I did, of course, assume there would be some career waiting for me down the road; I wasn't a complete buffoon. But I wasn't sure what shape it would take. Nor did I particularly care.

I began caring, however, as time went along, certainly after finishing my master's at Blah University, but especially during my doctoral work at Preppie. That development is hard to describe because there was never a moment when I woke up and said, "I think I'll become a world-renowned scholar instead of a student." But over the years, something like that began to take root. And if there was any one particular ingredient that especially nurtured such a thought, it was academic success: high praise for papers well written. Good grades from professors who had a tough reputation. Strategically planted suggestions from fellow graduate students and professors alike—about the best schools, the status jobs, the most money, the fast track. And most seductive of all, the insinuation that the distance between such grand objectives and my current performance was not a great one.

Under the influence of success, therefore, it was not long before I began fleshing out a future for myself. And of course, it was a future that involved a university of about Preppie's stature (or better), a position that was devoted primarily to research and a reward system that included a fair measure of privilege and

212

prestige. In other words, with each bit of well-meaning encouragement, I began to think increasingly of the possibilities attendant to the academic star system and the prospect of my being there. And with every such thought, there was a commensurate growth in the dimensions of my head and a corresponding constriction in the size of my heart.

By the time I entered the fourth year of graduate school, then, I was fully absorbed in the fast-lane values of academic achievement. Gone was the joy of cracking Durkheim. In its place was constant worry about rank, incessant talk about job options, and interminable ruminations about who was who—not only in the larger world of scholarship but also among my peers in the department. And interestingly enough, I hated it. Not the A's and accolades, certainly; I loved every minute of the applause. But I disliked intensely the notion that my success depended on the failure of others (which is the nature of external rewards), that if I got the highest grade in class, no one else could. That if I got the job at Cornell, no one else would. That if my paper was accepted for publication, someone else's would not be.

Most especially, I did not like losing the joy of cracking Durkheim. And that more than anything eventually led me to give up my fast-lane aspirations. Two events combined to bring about this change of heart. The first was the writing of my dissertation, which from all accounts is supposed to be one of the most miserable experiences of one's graduate career. But it wasn't for me. It was one of the best. I was fascinated by my chosen topic. I enjoyed researching it. And I found the writing of this, my first book-length manuscript, to be a genuine pleasure. Now this doesn't mean I was happy all the time. Happiness for me has very little to do with joy. Indeed, the process was steeped in pain and often unearthed imponderable questions and screams of anguish. But taken altogether, the pain, the questions, and the anguish constituted a grand existential fact. And that fact got me out of bed early every morning, filled my life with wonder and amazement and meaning. And brought back the joy that had hit me for the first time as a college undergraduate.

All of which must sound odd to everyone else, for whom I understand writing a dissertation is akin to passing a porcupine. But there you are. That's the way it was with me. And it happened at exactly the same time that a second important event occurred, the great purge of non-tenured faculty from my department. Somehow during my first few years at Preppie I had managed to ignore the negative effects of the external reward system. But around the beginning of my fourth year something happened that always happens at prestigious universities: Ninety percent of the young faculty got the boot to make room for a new squadron of non-tenured professors. In other words, it's an extraordinarily competitive system from which only a privileged few faculty emerge intact. But the most preposterous thing about this process was that the one or two faculty who "emerged intact" were not the scholars but the producers. They were the ones who had a knack for getting a research article published, but on the whole, they were not the faculty who either communicated well with students nor who seemed to understand the broader value of their own work. The real students, from my perspective, were the ones who were terminated.

Again, I am sure this is not always the case. Clearly, some very good scholars also get tenure at the best universities. But if they do, I discovered, it is not because of the depth of their wisdom but in spite of it. For it is neither wisdom nor brilliance nor teaching excellence that matters there. What matters is what you've published, where you've published it, and what others who have survived the system think about what you've published. And when I put that fact together with the enjoyment I was having working on my dissertation, it suddenly dawned on me that I was heading in quite the wrong direction. For I wanted to pursue the research that interested me, not the topics that were deemed legitimate by the academic power structure. I wanted to teach and enjoy the teaching process, not consider students an abscess or a necessary evil. Most of all, I wanted to be a scholar of the heart, pursuing those issues that were worth caring about, and doing it in a way the heart's Creator would find honorable, and its owner, delightful.

And so I made a decision. Without talking with anyone in the department, and after much prayer and discussion with Judy, I decided to look for a position at a small Christian liberal arts college of good repute, much like the one I had attended as an undergraduate. The kind of college that had nurtured (and put up with) me. The kind of college that was not afraid to involve the heart. And to make a long story short, within a few months of that decision, such a position opened up, and I was interviewed for and offered the job. And I accepted.

Not before the ink on the contract was dry, however, the department chairman at Preppie called me into his office. I couldn't imagine why he wanted to see me since he was not on my dissertation committee and I was working pretty independently at that time. I also felt somewhat guilty about going off and securing my own job without consulting anyone in the department. Guilty and a bit worried, since I knew they wanted their graduate students to land the best positions possible and expected to be involved in the search process. I had this gnawing suspicion, then, that I had failed to act according the department's standards and that I would be in trouble once someone found out about it. And that, combined with the nondefinitive nature of this office visit, made me more than a tad nervous as I walked into his office.

"Well Stan," he said as he pointed to a chair on the other side of his desk, "how are you these days? I haven't seen much of you lately." His eyes were bright, and he had the look of a man who had just finished a filet mignon. He was obviously in a good mood, in other words, and I immediately began to relax. It was a mistake.

"Oh, fine, Professor Vital," I said as I made my way over to the designated spot. "I've been holed up in my office for a while now, working on my dissertation mostly."

CHAPTER 8

"Good," he intoned nonchalantly as he picked up a paper and began studying it. "How is the project coming along, do you suppose?"

"Well, fine, I think," I stated hesitantly, knowing that was not my assessment to make. "I have completed the data analysis already and am well along in the writing."

"Yes," he looked up, breaking into a satisfied grin. "I've heard reports along those lines, Stan. Excellent reports. Keep up the good work." He got up from the chair behind his desk and took the seat across from me. Looking as if he was a man searching for precisely the right words, he began talking again.

"Stan, . . . I've got an opportunity for you. Quite unusual opportunity, to be precise. My good friend, Very Vital at Prima Preppie University, is looking for someone to fill a sociology of religion slot this coming spring. The position came up quickly, and he needs to fill it immediately for political reasons. He's not going to go through the usual search process, therefore. He'll make the appointment himself. Of course, it's not a tenure-track position at this point. It's a three-year slot. But I can tell you, on the sly, that whoever fills this will have a shot at a tenure-track position—if they merit consideration, of course . . . ," he added, regaining his professional composure.

"Anyway, Stan," he continued, returning his former grin, "I have nominated you for the position. And to be honest with you, I think you're a shoe-in for the job. Your research interests line up perfectly with their needs. You're already publishing. You have a good track record here as a teacher. And you're far enough along on your dissertation that you could start this spring. It's just a great fit."

An awkward pause followed thereafter, for he clearly expected some response from me, and I clearly didn't know what to say. Finally, out of sheer discomfort, I said, "Thank you," or something to that effect, after which he began to talk some more. "You do understand what an opportunity this is, don't you Stan?" he intoned, as he leaned forward and peered directly in my eyes.

SUCCESS

"Why if this position were being filled next fall, they would have five hundred applicants for it at least. You can't do better than this coming right out of grad school, you know. . . ."

I managed to leave his office having made no commitments and no confessions. In fact, I don't think I said anything whatsoever except "thank you," and I'm sure he must have been wondering how he could have tapped such an inarticulate young man for such an esteemed position. But I didn't know what else to do, so stunned was I by this sudden turn of events and so thoroughly aware of the awkward position I now found myself in.

What was I going to do? That question swirled around in my head as I jumped on my bike and headed down the road toward our apartment. On the surface, there was the problem of the signed contract. I had already committed myself to another position at another college. But deep down inside, I knew that wasn't a huge problem since I assumed the college would not hold me to the contract if I called them immediately. After all, they hadn't even received the contract in the mail yet. And besides, I was dealing with fellow Christians. I knew they would understand.

But that meant the problem I faced wasn't really what I had already obligated myself to, but what choice I should make about my future. Before my meeting with Professor Vital, my future had been clear. I didn't want a university position. I wanted to teach in a liberal arts college. The offer from Professor Vital, however, seemed to throw that reasoning into question. Now I had a bird in the hand, after all. Before I didn't know if I could land a university job even if I tried. Not only that, now I was being offered a prime position. Before such a job was not even in the realm of possibility. Now the bright light of achievement glowed brighter than it had ever glowed before, empowered by the confidence of my professors and the knowledge that success was actually within my grasp.

And then there was something else. If I said, "No thanks," at this point, I was cutting myself off—not only from the opportu-

217

nity of a lifetime—but also from the admiration, if not the certification of my professors. What would they think of my decision? And how would that affect their evaluation of me as well as my dissertation? I was jeopardizing more than a high status career, in other words. I was throwing my academic future at Preppie into question.

When I arrived back at the apartment, Heather was taking her afternoon nap and Judy was deep in a book (and deep in the couch as well). Not being mindful of her condition, I immediately launched into a description of the entire day's events and the horrendous bind I felt I was in. She listened intently, as she always does, even though I had no doubt yanked her right out of the Middle Ages. When I had finished complaining and silence finally descended upon the room, she looked at me with those always caring, always comforting eyes, but this time they had just a little edge to them.

"Well, Stan," she said, looking out the window for a second and then back in my direction, "I'm not sure what to say. I mean, I'm not sure whether to congratulate you or console you. You sound like you want to be consoled, but . . ."

It was uncharacteristically Judy, and I resented the implication that my complaints were less than wholehearted.

"Congratulations has nothing to do with it," I snapped. "I don't need compliments. I need help!"

A few minutes of silence followed thereafter, Judy looking down at her book and me trying to figure out why Judy's reaction was so different from what I expected, and so different from mine.

"Well," Judy finally broke in, "I'm not sure about that. . . ." She stopped and looked over at me, "But if that's the case, then we have some praying to do, don't we?"

"Yah," I muttered halfheartedly as I picked myself up out of my seat and walked over to my desk. And of course I was deeply offended by the suggestion. After all, what I was looking for was comfort, not questions about my motives. And definitely not suggestions concerning my piety. I sank down into my seat, burying my head in my hands, and began to pray. It was an act of desperation, not obedience, and I don't remember doing anything in the first part of my prayer besides carrying on with the complaints that I had begun with my wife. *Maybe the Lord will be consoling even if my wife isn't,* I thought.

Somewhere in the midst of my prayer, however, a voice came out of the other room carrying the simple message, "I love you." It was a message I had often heard before—in the morning, at night, and sometimes in the silence that ensues after an argument. I didn't respond. Judy's "I love yous" don't require a response, for one thing. They have enough integrity to stand on their own. But I was praying, for another, and so I just continued my conversation with the Lord. Nevertheless, the impact of that "I love you" on my prayer was profound, releasing me from self-doubt and self-absorption, and enabling me to begin pursuing issues of greater importance. Like what the Lord really desired of me. And the age-old question of the Lord's will, that question that had so plagued me from the very beginning of our trip back east.

The Lord's will. *Were we back to that again?* I thought. Surely not, I muttered to myself. The will of the Lord is to do what is good and right and consistent with his Word, and leave the rest in the Lord's hands. I knew that. So the question was, what did I know to be right? And what remained to be properly placed in the hands of the Lord?

And then it struck me like a ton of bricks that I had, once again, reversed the equation. That, on the one hand, I was spending my time praying that the Lord would help me to make the right decision when I already knew what the right decision was. And that, on the other, I was taking the future upon myself, worrying about the consequences of whatever decision I might make, even though I didn't have a snowball's chance of controlling the events that were yet to come. And what was the right decision? It was the one I had made long before the value of success entered the picture, when I had freely determined that a university position was not good for me. And what was the thing that now caused me

CHAPTER 8

so much distress, over which I had no control? It was the future. My future at Preppie if I said, "No thanks." My future as an academic, if I turned my back on the world's definition of success.

Shaking my head in disbelief, it suddenly dawned on me that I really didn't need to spend an hour agonizing in prayer before the Lord. I only needed to ask for the strength and courage to do what was right, and to put the consequences in the Lord's hands. To join the battle on the right side, in other words, and trust the Lord to take care of me in the midst of the fight.

"Well, Partner," came soft words from directly behind me, perfectly coordinated with a shoulder massage and dripping with acceptance, "what's it going to be? Prima Preppie or that smaaaaaall Christian college up north? Shall we go for success, my friend? Or shall we go for broke?"

"As if you didn't already know." I turned around with a mock frown and buried my head in her arms. "You might just as well have asked me to choose between right and wrong."

"Oh," she said as she commenced with a head scratch, "I guess I thought I had." It was said with affection, and that's the way I heard it. And so we just held each other for a while until I started to lose circulation in my left ear.

"What do you say, Hon," I said, as I pulled back and gave my ear a breather. "Shall we pass on this invitation to join the fast track and stay to the Right instead?"

"I thought you'd never ask," she said as she led me over to the couch.

"I'll bet the Lord wondered the same thing," I mumbled as I obediently and eagerly followed behind.